Walks on the Lleyn Peninsula

The Lleyn Coastal Path near Mynydd Gwyddel

Walks on the Lleyn Peninsula

Sixteen circular walks exploring the coast and hills

Carl Rogers

Mara Books

First published in April 1999 by **Mara Books**,
22 Crosland Terrace, Helsby, Cheshire WA6 9LY.
Telephone: 01928 723744

This new fully revised edition published by
Mara Books, March 2006.

ISBN 1 902512 00 6

All enquiries regarding sales, telephone: (01928) 723744

Acknowledgements:

I would like to thank Jack Rogers, Audrey Rogers and Bob Nash for their help in revising this book.

Layout and design by Mara Books.

British Library Cataloguing-in-publication data.

A catalogue is available for this book from the British Library.

Whilst every effort has been made to ensure that the information in this book is correct, the author or the publisher can accept no responsibility for errors, loss or injury however caused.

Maps based on out of copyright Ordnance Survey mapping.

Contents

A map of Lleyn showing the location of the walks

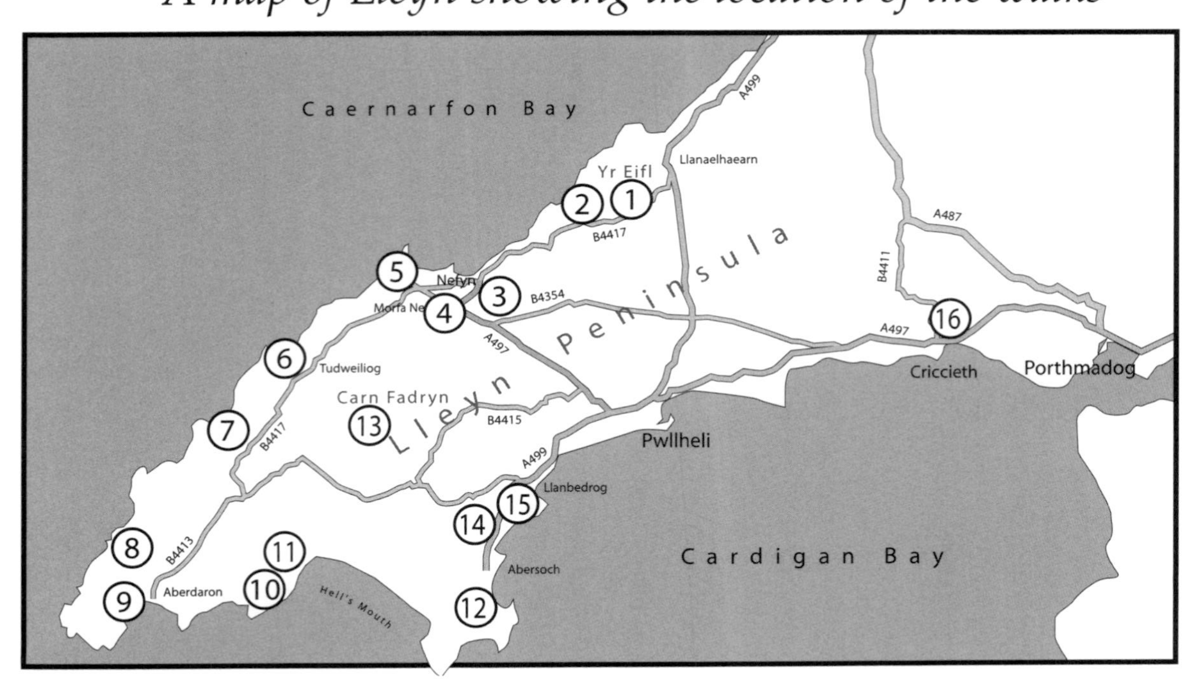

Introduction

THE Lleyn Peninsula reaches west from the mountainous heartland of Snowdonia to form both the northern limit of Cardigan Bay and the southern arc of Caernarfon Bay to the north. It is the northern-most and smallest of the three great peninsulas which dominate the western coastline of England and Wales—Lleyn, Pembrokeshire and Cornwall.

Despite sharing many characteristics with these larger cousins, Lleyn has its own very distinct character which also sets it apart from the rest of Wales. It is composed mainly of flat low-lying farmland—but what would otherwise be a rather monotonous landscape has been transformed by a generous scattering of shapely volcanic hills which run along its length like a backbone and give it an unmistakeable skyline when viewed from across the waters of Cardigan Bay, or from the western seaboard of Anglesey.

Its two coastlines are very different. The north coast—which embraces the southern arc of Caernarfon Bay and receives the full force of westerly winds—is characterised by low cliffs and occasional wide sandy bays. It is very much 'off the beaten track' and makes ideal walking country having an almost continuous coastal path. There are no large towns or resorts and its beaches are quiet for much of the time.

The south coast is a complete contrast. A line of resorts stretch from Abersoch to Porthmadog and its sheltered beaches are busy throughout the holiday season. Pwllheli is the capital of the area and is also the terminus of the rail line from Porthmadog. There is a sizeable harbour, supermarkets and even a holiday camp. Further west is the up-market resort of Abersoch, sporting perhaps the finest stretch of sand in Lleyn. Its sheltered bay is busy throughout the holiday season with water skiers and yachtsmen and exclusive chalet developments line the bay.

Lleyn even has its own 'Land's End', along with perhaps the

most famous holy island in Wales—Ynys Enlli or Bardsey. The coastline between Abersoch and Bardsey is among the most dramatic in North Wales, with spectacular cliff scenery and some of the most treacherous coastal waters in Britain. Porth Neigwl or Hell's Mouth as it is better known, is one of the most famous shipping black spots in the country. This four-mile-wide bay, enclosed by high rocky headlands, faces the prevailing wind and became the grave of literally hundreds of ships during the age of sail.

Although the interior of Lleyn is flat and low lying for the most part, it is far from dull and uninteresting. Several steep sided volcanic hills run throughout its length giving grand views of the surrounding coastline and inland to the mountains of Snowdonia which more than compensates for their low altitude.

Like Anglesey, Lleyn has a relatively mild and dry climate and often hours of sunshine can be enjoyed here when the highlands of Snowdonia are draped in mist and rain. It may also be easier to avoid the crowds on some of the wilder stretches of coastline, particularly away from the summer months when the walking is often better. Crisp clear days in the autumn and spring will give the best walking conditions, while it is worth remembering that many of the less frequented paths will be overgrown with bracken in the late summer. The winter months can often be wet and extremely windy making stretches of the coastal path dangerous.

A brief history of Lleyn

THROUGHOUT man's history in Britain, Lleyn has been attractive to settlers. This is particularly true of the prehistoric period when the mountainous hinterland of Snowdonia did not isolate it as it does today. The reason for this is that throughout much of this period—when the main method of travel was by sea rather land—Lleyn lay on a major communication route and is known to have been populated long before the interior of Britain became accessible. As evidence of this, both Lleyn and adjacent Anglesey abound in prehistoric remains which date from man's earliest settlement in these islands.

Earliest of these are the various burial chambers which now

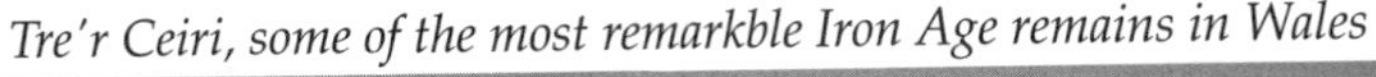

Tre'r Ceiri, some of the most remarkble Iron Age remains in Wales

stand isolated in fields or on lonely hillsides. Much of their original structure has been stripped away by the elements leaving the familiar *'tumulus'*—the chamber which held the body or cremated remains. One of the most important finds from this period in Lleyn is the stone axe factory on the slopes of Mynydd Rhiw (route 11). Tools produced here have been found as far away as Gwent, suggesting a fairly advanced trading infastructure.

The next phase of settlement is known as the Bronze Age and began towards the end of the second millennium BC when tribes—who have become known as the Beaker People from the distinctive pottery urns used to hold the cremated remains of their dead—arrived in Britain. They brought with them the knowledge of metal working and raised the enigmatic standing stones to be seen all over Britain. Around 500 BC, restless Iron Age tribes arrived in Britain from the Continent and with them came the knowledge of working a new metal—iron. These people were the Celts, ancestors of the modern day Welsh and were the people who faced the Romans in the early decades of the first century. It was during the Celtic period that the great hillforts were built and examples are to be seen enclosing the summits of almost every hill in the district. Lleyn has one of the most impressive and well preserved examples of an Iron Age hill fort in the country, Tre'r Ceiri, which encloses one of the peaks in the Yr Eifl group (route 1). A similar though less imposing structure can be seen on the summit of Garn Boduan, near Nefyn (route 3).

The Roman occupation of Britain left very few remains in Lleyn, although their main fort in North Wales lies close by at Segontium (Caernarfon), with a second fortress at Tomen-y-Mur near Trawsfynydd. Evidence of a smaller camp has also been found at Dolbenmaen a few miles to the north of Criccieth and the scant remains of a bathhouse have been unearthed at Tremadog, but that seems to be about it. Like Anglesey, no Roman roads have been uncovered in Lleyn, leading to the conclusion that the area had little or no military importance to the Romans (roads generally linked forts). Any travelling carried out in the area would thus have been along native tracks already in existence.

In the post Roman era, with Britain left undefended, Irish invaders seized the opportunity to overrun and establish settlements in much of western Wales. Lleyn, as the nearest point to Ireland (and often within sight of it) must have suffered badly at this time as did nearby Anglesey. The colonisation was finally halted and the Irish expelled by a Celtic chieftain who came to Wales from one of the northern British kingdoms (who were to disappear totally in the following centuries). His name was Cunedda and he brought with him a large band of warriors said to have been led by his sons. The Irish were finally defeated in a last battle in Anglesey around 470 AD. After his death Cunedda's

Iron Age hut circles at Tre'r Ceiri

sons each ruled part of what would eventually become the kingdom of Gwynedd.

While the Irish were harassing the west of Britain and the Picts from beyond Hadrian's Wall were causing trouble in the north, Saxons from the Continent were making raids along the east coast. The British high king at that time was Vortigern and in an attempt to control these invasions he is said to have enlisted the help of Saxon mercenaries. The ploy worked at first but the inevitable happened. The Saxons turned on their employer and began to take land for themselves and establish their own kingdoms. The British fought against them but their colonisation, unlike that of the Irish, could not be halted. Vortigern was blamed and fled but was pursued and some say killed. The refuge where his enemies are said to have finally caught up with him is Nant Gwrtheyrn, an isolated valley at the foot of Yr Eifl in northeast Lleyn (route 2). Vortigern is remembered today in the valley's name; Nant Gwrtheyrn, which means 'Vortigern's Valley'.

By the early sixth century most of the Celtic tribes in Britain had been converted to Christianity and missionary priests were touring the land preaching to and converting the remaining

Bardsey Island (Ynys Enlli)

inhabitants. Many of the present village names commemorate the names of these priests. They are identified today by the word *'llan'* which appears at the beginning of the name and refers to an early church foundation, followed by the name of the priest or 'saint' who founded it (eg. Llanbedrog is the *'llan'* of Pedrog).

Lleyn's greatest claim to fame during the Dark Age period is undoubtedly the pilgrimage to Bardsey, where a monastic settlement had been established as early as 516 AD by Celtic priests from Brittany. By this time the Irish threat was but a faint memory and the western seaboard of Wales was sheltered from the threat posed by the expanding Saxon kingdoms in the east. Many priests fled to Wales and the west became known as a place of sanctuary. In the following century monks escaping from the aftermath of the Battle of Chester in 616 AD, where over 1,000 monks from the nearby abbey are said to have been slaughtered by Northumbrian Saxons, also came here seeking refuge. So arduous was their journey through what is now Snowdonia, enduring its harsh mountain terrain and wild animals, that it took on great religious significance. Bardsey seems to have attracted so many 'holy men' in the following centuries who came here to end their days, that it is reputed to be the burial place of over '20,000 saints'. Bardsey remained the goal of pilgrims for several hundred years and the route through Lleyn became known as the 'Pilgrims' Road'. Three trips to Bardsey were said to equal one to Rome.

Before the Edwardian conquest of Wales the quarrels of its numerous princes and the ensuing conflicts must have touched the lives of Lleyn's inhabitants on many occasions. Lleyn came under the rulership of Gwynedd and Gruffydd ap Cynan, one of its most notable rulers is known to have used a castle at Nefyn as a base in his struggle for control of Gwynedd in the eleventh century. He was given sanctuary at Aberdaron after his escape from Norman imprisonment at Chester Castle. Here he was provided with a boat which took him to Ireland before his victorious return.

The twelfth century traveller Gerald of Wales passed through Lleyn and reports that a hilltop fortress on Carn Fadryn (route 13) was held by the 'sons of Qwain', a reference to Qwain Gwynedd, another notable ruler of Gwynedd. Nothing remains of this fortress today but Lleyn does have one castle which has survived more or less intact—Criccieth (route 16). This castle is notable in being the only one of Edward I's Welsh castles to be built on an earlier native foundation. Much of the inner castle was built by probably the greatest of all the Welsh princes, Llywelyn ap Iowerth, known as 'Llywelyn the Great' or 'Llywelyn Fawr'. He was the first Welsh prince to unify the various warring factions within Wales, something which had not happened since the Romans had left. He built Criccieth about ten years before his death in 1240 and used it to imprison his eldest son, the illegitimate Gruffydd whom he did not favour as his successor. Gruffydd eventually died in a fall while trying to escape from the Tower of London where he had been held by Henry III after being handed over by his brother Dafydd. After Dafydd's short rule the succession reverted to the alternative line. Gruffydd's son Llywelyn rose next to become almost as famous as his grandfather. He had the added distinction of becoming the last independent prince of Wales. He was finally overthrown after a long power struggle by Edward I and was killed at Builth Wells in 1282.

Edward celebrated his conquest of Wales with a tournament at Nefyn, possibly one of the most important events to take place in Lleyn. He then embarked on a programme of castle building to enable the English kings to keep the Welsh in subjection. He improved the defences at Criccieth and built castles at nearby Harlech and Caernarfon. Criccieth Castle was finally put out of service by the rebels of Owain Glyndŵr and has been a ruin ever since.

After the time of Glyndŵr, Lleyn left the national stage along with much of Wales. The fifteenth to the eighteenth centuries saw most activity directed into agriculture; mainly cattle raising on the low grade land which makes up the majority of the interior, and fishing for herring in the stormy seas which surround Lleyn. Thomas Pennant mentioned the herring fisheries towards the end of the eighteenth century and suggested that it was this activity which was responsible for the poor state of agriculture in Lleyn.

The sea remained important to the inhabitants of Lleyn throughout the eighteenth, nineteenth and early twentieth centuries. Early in this period Pwllheli developed as a centre for fishing and ship building and remained prominent until it was eclipsed by the rapid rise of Porthmadog following the reclamation schemes of William Alexander Madocks at Traeth Mawr. On the opposite coast a tiny sea port was bracing itself for great things, particularly as Madocks' embankment across

Porth Dinllaen

Traeth Mawr had solved one of North Wales' major communication problems. The dangerous crossing of the tidal estuary of Afon Glaslyn was now a thing of the past and moves were afoot to improve the road through mid Wales. The newly formed Porth Dinllaen Harbour Company banked on the success of a parliamentary bill to make Porth Dinllaen the packet port for Ireland. In the end it was defeated by just one vote.

The loss of trade to Holyhead left the tiny port frozen in time and so it has remained. However, we only need to look at Holyhead today and the development along the North Wales coast to see what the effect would have been on Lleyn had things turned out differently.

Madocks' town of Tremadog lay on the line of the proposed road to the new port and would have made large profits catering for those travelling to and from Ireland. The loss of this trade has kept Tremadog almost in its original form, but the building of Madocks' sea wall created a new opportunity. The diversion of Afon Glaslyn carved out a new deep water channel and a small port was soon built on the reclaimed land. This grew quickly to serve the slate quarries at Blaenau Ffestiniog which were being developed by Samuel Holland at the time. A narrow gauge railway was constructed to bring stone to Porthmadog and for almost half a century it was one of the busiest ports in Wales.

A rapid fall in the demand for slate brought an end to its prosperity in the early 1900s. By then its ship building was also waning but within a few decades it found new prosperity as a tourist destination. The excellent beaches and sheltered inland water of the estuary have proved popular with holiday makers and the summer months will find the streets busier than ever. This is also true of most of Lleyn although agriculture is still important, particularly away from the coast.

Glossary of Welsh names

Aber ....*river mouth*
Abaty ....*abbey*
Afon ....*river*
Bach ....*little*
Bryn ....*hill, eminence*
Cae ....*field, enclosure*
Caer ....*fort*
Canol ....*middle*
Capel ....*chapel*
Carn, Carnedd ....*heap of stones*
Carreg ....*crag or stone*
Castell ....*castle or fortress*
Cefn ....*ridge*
Clogwyn ....*cliff*
Coch ....*red*
Coed ....*wood*
Cors ....*bog or swamp*
Craig ....*crag*
Croes/Groes ....*cross*
Cwm ....*coombe*
Dinas ....*city, fortress*
Ddu ....*black*
Dyffryn ....*valley*
Eglwys ....*church*
Eryri ....*highland*
Esgair ....*ridge*
Fach ....*small*
Faes ....*meadow*
Fawr ....*large*
Felin ....*mill*
Ffordd ....*road*
Ffynnon ....*well or fountain*
Foel ....*bare hill*
Gaer ....*camp*
Galt ....*slope*
Glas ....*blue-green*
Glyn ....*deep valley*
Goch ....*red*
Gors ....*swamp*
Grach ....*scabby*
Gwyn ....*white*
Hafod ....*summer dwelling*
Hen ....*old*
Isaf ....*lower*
Llan ....*church*
Llyn ....*lake*
Llys ....*hall or court*
Lon ....*lane*
Maen ....*stone*
Maes ....*field or meadow*
Mawr ....*large*
Moel ....*rounded hill*
Mor ....*sea*
Morfa ....*flat seashore, sea fen*
Mynach ....*monk*
Mynydd ....*mountain*
Newydd ....*new*
Ogof ....*cave*
Pant ....*hollow*
Parc ....*park*
Pen ....*head or point*
Penrhyn ....*promontory*
Pentre ....*village*
Pistyll ....*waterfall*
Plas ....*house*
Pont ....*bridge*
Porth ....*port*
Pwll ....*pool*
Rhos...................................*moorland*
Rhyd ....*ford*
Sarn ....*causeway*
Tomen ....*mound*
Traeth ....*beach, sandy shore*
Tref ....*town*
Trwyn...............................*peninsula*
Twll ....*cavern*
Twr ....*tower*
Ty ....*house*
Tyddyn ....*farmstead*
Uchaf ....*upper*
Waun ....*moorland*
Wen ....*white*
Wern/Gwern ....*alder swamp*
Y, Yr ....*the*
Yn ....*in*
Ynys ....*island*

WALK 1

Yr Eifl (The Rivals)

Distance: *3 miles*

There are few places in Lleyn which escape the dramatic profile of Yr Eifl. Seen from the south or west across the pastoral interior they rise as a series of purple cones. From the Caernarfon road they tower above the village of Trefor, and from the graceful bay at Porth Dinllaen they cascade into the sea. Yet the highest top is just 1,850 feet (564m) and little more than half the height of nearby Snowdon.

This walk explores the two most interesting tops—the highest summit and Tre'r Ceiri, site of the finest Iron Age remains in Wales. The ascents are moderately strenuous though fairly short as the starting point is already 856ft. Footpaths are food throughout although a little faint here and there.

Start: From Llanaelhaearn (on the Caernarfon to Pwllheli road) the B4417 rises steeply to 856 feet before dropping to the village of Llithfaen. Just beyond this high point, a narrow lane bears to the left and a few cars may be parked on the verge.
Grid ref: 367 434 (Landranger 123, Explorer 253).

The walk

1. Go through the old iron kissing gate opposite (on the north side of the road) and head directly up the sloping field towards Caergribin, a prominent castellated rock on the skyline. Higher up a ladder stile leads onto the open heather covered moors. As you approach Caergribin the path curves left around the rocks.

Our next objective, Tre'r Ceiri, can be clearly seen now rising to the northeast with its encircling walls. A narrow footpath leads through the heather soon bearing left to join a more prominent path coming up from Llithfean at a T junction. Turn right here and a little further on cross a stone wall by a large ladder stile. As you approach the final slopes of Tre'r Ceiri keep left at a fork and make the final rise. Enter the enclosure through the obvious entrance at the southwestern end just above the information board and make your way through the hut circles on the right-hand edge of the enclosure to the highest point.

Once on the summit you will see that your climb has been well rewarded; not only are you greeted by one of the finest panoramas in Lleyn, but you have before you the most impressive and well preserved Iron Age remains in Wales.

Here you will need little imagination to visualise the settlement as it was, the site is remarkably well preserved and this, along with its vast size may have given rise to the name—Tre'r Ceiri—which means 'town of the giants'. The outer walls, some six feet thick and up to fifteen feet high, enclose an area almost 900 feet by 400 feet, and are composed entirely of dry stone walling. Within this are the remains of some 150 hut circles of varying size and shape, all well preserved. Of particular note is the survival of the walls almost to their original height. A wall walk and parapet which enabled defenders to patrol the walls is also in amazingly good repair.

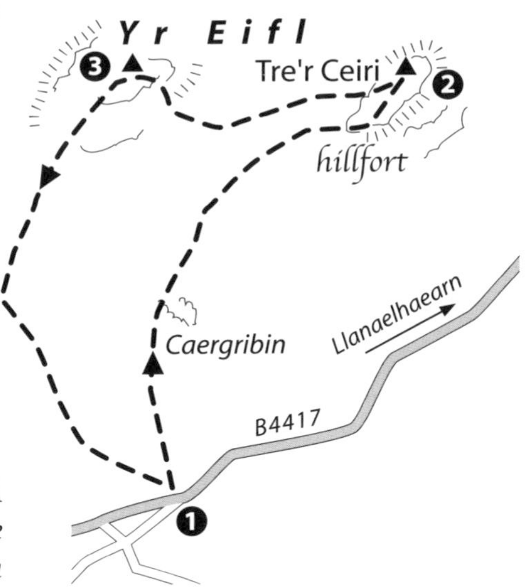

The ruins are thought to date from the mid-second century AD although finds suggest that occupation continued until the end of the fourth century AD. A Bronze Age cairn within the enclosure indicates even

earlier use of the site—common with many other hill forts. Some of these sites may have been inhabited continuously throughout the Bronze Age and Iron Age—a period of perhaps 1,000 years or more.

2. From the summit walk north (towards Caernarfon Bay) and bear left to walk beside the wall. Pass a tunnelled exit in the wall and continue to a second paved entrance above the col between Tre'r Ceiri and the main summit of Yr Eifl. Leave the enclosure here and bear right to exit through a gap in the lower wall. Turn right immediately and follow a faint footpath which soon curves leftwards through the heather with the main summit directly ahead.

As the hillside becomes steeper, the path turns diagonally-leftwards eventually joining the main footpath which rises steeply from the left. (Alternatively, reach this point by returning to the stone wall crossed earlier and follow the main path which ascends the hillside to the right).

Turn right and make the short rise to the summit.

As one would expect the panorama from the highest summit in the group is extensive taking in much of Lleyn's cultivated landscape. The closeness of the sea here exaggerates the height of these little 'mountains' which fall over 1,800 feet to the waters of Caernarfon Bay.

These steep northern slopes guard the secluded valley of Nant Gwrtheyrn; traditionally held to be the final retreat of Vortigern, the exiled British king who lost control of his kingdom to the Saxons in the fifth century. His troubles arose as the result of an attempt to enlist the help of Saxon mercenaries to defend his kingdom from the Picts and Irish. His plan worked at first but things turned against him when the Saxons broke the terms of their treaty and began to seize lands and establish their own kingdoms.

Vortigern is said to have fled to North Wales and sought refuge in this remote valley from his own people. Today the valley still bears his name—Nant Gwrtheyrn means 'Vortigern's Valley'.

3. From the triangulation pillar a path descends southwest, initially between two small ridges of broken rocks, then through

Approaching Tre'r Ceiri from Caergribin

heather with the village of Llithfaen directly ahead. Lower down as the angles begins to ease cross the faint remains of a drystone wall running at right angles to the path (this is visible from higher up on the hillside). Turn left here and follow a narrow path which runs beside the stone wall with the green dome of Mynydd Garnguwch (the hill with the pimple-like cairn on its summit) rising directly ahead.

Keep ahead where the wall disappears and cross a path which leads down to a cottage by pines on the right. Further on you meet a track which also leads down to the cottage seen previously. The track forks here. Take the right-hand fork which is straight ahead as you approach. This track shortly runs into fields where

Yr Eifl from the west

an old iron ladder stile crosses the fence by a gate. The right of way follows the edge of a depression or gully running through the centre of the field. Follow this and just before a wall corner, bear left, cross the gully and head across the field. Aim for a gate in the far fence which soon becomes visible. Continue through the following field to the kissing gate used at the beginning of the walk.

WALK 2

Nant Gwrtheyrn

Distance: *3½ miles*

This is a hill walk in reverse. Part of the new Lleyn Coastal Path is used to descend into the hidden, isolated valley of Nant Gwrtheyrn—one of the most remarkable locations in Lleyn. Hemmed in on three sides by the sheer walls of Yr Eifl (The Rivals), the only escape from the valley is by one of the steepest roads in Wales. Footpaths are good throughout and waymarked for the Lleyn Coastal Path.

Start: There is a sizable car park and picnic area below Yr Eifl on the road which runs north from Llithfaen to Nant Gwrtheyrn. *Grid ref: 353 440 (Landranger 123, Explorer 253).*

The walk

1. Turn right out of the car park and after about 100 yards bear right onto a bridleway (sign). After a short walk across open ground enter fields by a gate. Keep to the right beside the wall in the first two fields then, where the wall veers to the left, go through a small gate on the right and cut through the centre of the field to a gap in the remains of a stone wall with two cottages to the left.

Ahead, a fine view opens out of Lleyn's northern coast, with the prominent headland at Porth Dinllaen and the conical hill of Carn Fadryn clearly visible.

This section of footpath follows the old pilgrims' route to Bardsey from Clynnog Fawr which came over Bwlch Yr Eifl and continued on to Nefyn. It was used throughout the Middle Ages when the island attracted pilgrims from all over Britain. Three trips to Bardsey were said to equal one to Rome.

Drop to a gate and follow a faint grass track/path for about 200 yards before turning right through a small gate in the wall. Turn left beside the wall then, don't cross the next stile and wall, instead, bear right and follow the wall down to a farm track. Turn right and immediately right again at a fork following the track to 'Cilia Isaf', a small hill farm overlooking the sea.

If visibility is good, you will be able to pick out Holyhead Mountain and the yellow strip of sand at Newborough Warren on the west coast of Anglesey. As you continue, the dominant profile of the seaward Rival (Yr Eifl) comes into view dropping sheer to the sea. These impressive little peaks rise directly from the sea and appear far higher than they actually are.

Beyond the farm buildings bear left to a small gate then turn half-right onto a descending footpath. This is faint at first but soon becomes more established as it descends the hillside diagonally. Take care not to miss this, if a higher path is taken you will not be able to get down to the beach.

Once on the path it is easy to follow and should be waymarked as it is now part of the new Lleyn Coastal Path. Continue to the shingle beach where old machinery and the remains of quarrying activity litter the shore.

2. A good footpath rises from the stoney beach to the rebuilt village of Porth y Nant.

This little hamlet lies hidden in one of the most isolated valleys in Wales—Nant Gwrtheyrn. It is backed by the steep northern slopes of Yr Eifl which rise to over 1,800 feet and completely enclose the valley. To the north, all entry is prevented by high sea cliffs and the cold waters of Caernarfon Bay.

Nant Gwrtheyrn is associated in Welsh tradition with Vortigern, the exiled British high king, who is said to have sought refuge here in the closing years of the fifth century. Vortigern has the unenviable reputation for having initiated the Saxon conquest of England.

His story comes to us from the writings of Gildas, a sixth century cleric and Nennius, a ninth century historian. They tell us that Vortigern, who ruled from about 425-461 AD, was having trouble controlling the extremities of his kingdom and enlisted the help of Saxon mercenaries under two brothers, Hengist and Horsa, to fight the Picts, who were making raids south of Hadrian's Wall, and the Irish who were attacking the western seaboard of Britain.

The ploy worked at first but, having nothing with which to pay them Vortigern was forced to offer land (some sources say the Isle of Thanet) and supplies of food. After initial success, the Saxons became dissatisfied and broke the terms of their treaty on the grounds that their supplies were insufficient. They subsequently allied themselves with other Saxons from both Britain and their homeland and proceeded to lay waste Vortigern's kingdom 'from sea to sea'. After the initial attack their advance was checked for a while but the Britons then turned on Vortigern as a traitor and the Saxons were never to leave Britain again.

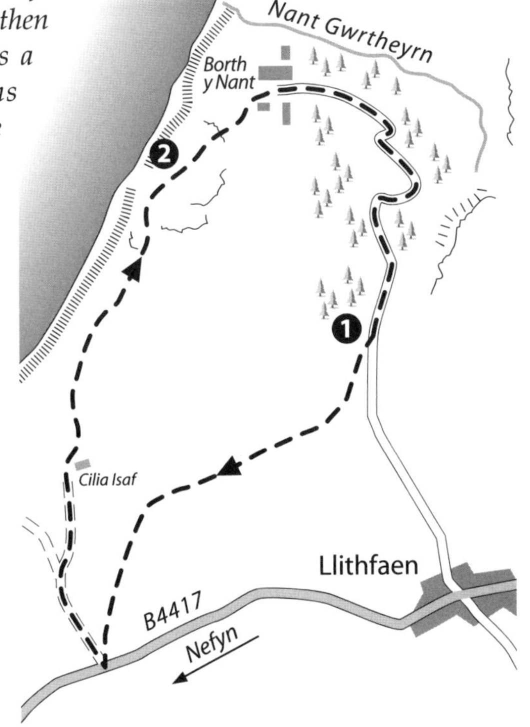

According to Welsh tradition, Vortigern was overthrown by Ambrosius (Emrys in Welsh) who had taken part in the resistance against Hengist and Horsa. He fled to North Wales where he tried to establish a stronghold at Dinas Emrys, near Beddgelert. Ambrosius again caught up with him and he came finally to this valley in a

Old winding gear on the beach near Porth y Nant

desperate bid to find refuge. Other stories claim that he was overtaken by his enemies and died in battle. Whatever his fate, the valley has since been known as Nant Gwrtheyrn meaning 'Vortigern's Valley'.

In more recent times, the valley enjoyed a brief period of prosperity from quarrying although it was relatively short lived. Quarrying began in about 1851 and in the following decade the nearby village of Porth y Nant was built to house the quarrymen. There were 24 houses, a co-operative shop and chapel. When the fortunes of the quarry waned the local population left, the last inhabitant leaving in 1959.

The decay of this village recalls an ancient legend which relates how, in the early years of the Dark Ages, three monks entered the valley in an attempt to convert its small community to Christianity. The locals did not take kindly to the preaching of the three monks and drove them out of the valley. As they neared the top of Yr Eifl they looked back and cursed the valley and its pagan inhabitants. "No one will ever receive burial in consecrated ground after death" declared one monk. "No male and female will ever be allowed to marry each other" came the second curse. Finally the third spoke, "the village will eventually decay and die".

The story goes on to relate how, in the centuries that followed the inhabitants met untimely deaths either from drowning or from falls from the nearby cliffs—the only means of living being the rearing of sheep and fishing— thus no one received a church burial. Also its young people, fearful of the curse invariably looked to other communities for marriage mates and left the valley. As a result the valley gradually became depopulated and the community died.

There is still no community here although the ruined buildings were renovated in 1978 and now house a Welsh National Language Centre.

Follow the road, which becomes extremely steep higher up, back to the car park at point 1.

(Part-way up the hill a footpath cuts through the trees on the left but it is better to stay on the road if only for the bird's eye view of the valley from the last bend.)

WALK 3

Garn Boduan & Mynydd Nefyn

Distance: *5 miles*

This walk starts with a stiff climb to the summit of Garn Boduan where you can enjoy superb views across much of Lleyn in clear weather. A return is made by a gentler ascent onto the open land and conifer plantations of Mynydd Nefyn. Footpaths are good throughout, particularly in the second half used by the new Lleyn Coastal Path.

Start: There is a small car park beside the old chapel off 'Stryd y Plas', (opposite the Aberdaron road B4417) in the centre of Nefyn. *Grid ref: 308 404 (Landranger 123, Explorer 253).*

The walk

1. Turn left out of the car park and in 20 yards or so bear right into 'Y Fron', a narrow dead end access road which soon begins to climb towards the woods of Garn Boduan. Higher up, the road becomes unsurfaced and eventually turns right by outbuildings towards a farm. Take the footpath up the bank directly ahead here. The path is sunken between low banks at first, then enters a field. Go ahead up the field edge and through a gateway in the top corner. Keep ahead through a smaller field to enter conifer woods by an old kissing gate hidden behind gorse bushes.

Turn right on a footpath through the trees. At the end of the path turn left to a T junction with a much broader path. Turn left here and follow this path up through the trees. At the top of the rise the trees thin out and a forest road joins from the left. Ignore this, taking the path ahead instead.

Climb steadily again and at the top of the next rise where the broad path bends left and starts to descend, take the narrow path ahead which rises steeply through the heather. Shortly the path levels at a rounded shoulder, then curves right below the final rocks. A little further on bear left between boulders to reach the highest point.

Like most of Lleyn's hills, Garn Boduan gives superb views in every direction despite its modest height. The main difference here is the extensive plateau-like summit, which may come as a surprise after such a steep climb. This made it an ideal retreat in times of trouble and like the more famous Tre'r Ceiri, contains extensive remains dating from the Iron Age and possibly early Dark Age periods. The main hillfort

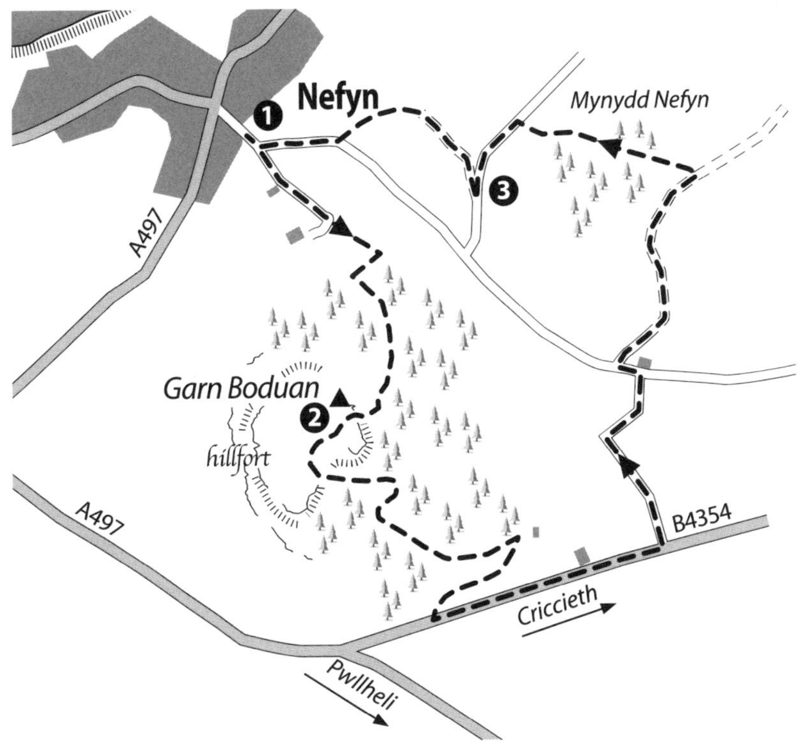

encloses an area of over 10 hectares and contains at least 170 hut circles. These can be seen covering the terraces to the west of the highest point. They are thought to represent several phases of settlement and would thus not all have been in use at one time.

Around the summit and to the southeast there is evidence of a much later structure, possibly as late as the seventh century as suggested by its name—Boduan means 'residence of Buan' a semi legendary figure from the period.

2. From the summit follow the path which heads southwest (directly towards Carn Fadryn). The path is narrow but visible and soon passes through an area of dead pine trunks and ruined drystone hut circles. A little further on the path curves leftwards above pines down to the right and below a craggy knoll on the left.

At a T junction with a broader path/track turn right and continue the descent to the next junction on a sharp bend with a forest road. Turn right here and follow this down to the road (B4354).

Turn left along the road and in 1/2 mile turn left again into a narrow lane signed to 'Mynydd Nefyn'. At the end of the lane turn left at the T junction and in 100 yards or so take the lane on the right. This leads up on to the open land of Mynydd Nefyn and you will soon have wide views to the right across the flat land of southeast Lleyn.

At a fork keep left (right fork leads to 'Parciau') eventually passing a cottage on the right ('Maes Glas'). After this continue along the rough lane to woods on the left where there is a fingerpost indicating the Lleyn Coastal Path. Turn left here over the stile and follow the path through the trees. In a 100 yards or so the path bears left, then takes a direct line through the thick conifer plantation.

As you emerge from the trees the path ahead is obvious and soon joins a forest track. Bear right along the track for about 30-40 yards before bearing left into the trees again on the obvious

Yr Eifl and Mynydd Nefyn from Garn Boduan

signed path. A little further on cross the track again taking the path ahead. Leave the woods by a gap in the wall and cross a rough bracken and gorse-covered field to enter a lane. Turn left along the lane.

3. After the first bend the lane begins to descend. In about 150 yards turn sharp right onto an access track signed for the coastal path.

There are wide views from this track down to Nefyn, Morfa Nefyn and Porth Dinllaen, isolated in its little headland.

Follow the track down to the gateway to 'Tal Ffolt'. Bear left here onto the narrow signed path which descends between old stone walls to a lane. Turn right here and return to Nefyn.

Nefyn

Distance: *$6^1/_4$ miles*

An easy walk mainly on the level through farmland, quiet lanes and along the coastal path high above Porth Nefyn. Care should be taken on this path. The boulder clay cliffs are suffering from coastal erosion and a section of path has been closed due to a land slip. At the time of writing a diversion is in operation.

Start: There is a sizable National Trust car park at the end of 'Lon Golff '(Golf Lane) in Morfa Nefyn.
Grid ref: 281 407 (Landranger 123, Explorer 253).

The walk

1. Return to the car park entrance and turn right along the road. At the end of the road where it enters the golf course, turn left between the clubhouse of 'Nefyn and District Golf Club' and 'RNLI House'. Pass between the buildings and walk ahead along a short track to enter fields by a kissing gate. Walk ahead along the field edge with Carn Fadryn directly ahead. Cross a farm access road by two kissing gates and continue ahead through the following field to a road on the edge of Edern village. Turn right down the hill into the village. Take the first road on the left in the centre of the village and after about 250 yards turn left onto a track which passes through the yard of 'Tyn Llan' farm. Follow the track past the church and cemetery and continue to cross a stream. Shortly the track turns sharp right–go through the kissing gate ahead here into fields.

Keep straight ahead along the field edge to cross a small stream by a footbridge. Walk directly across the following field

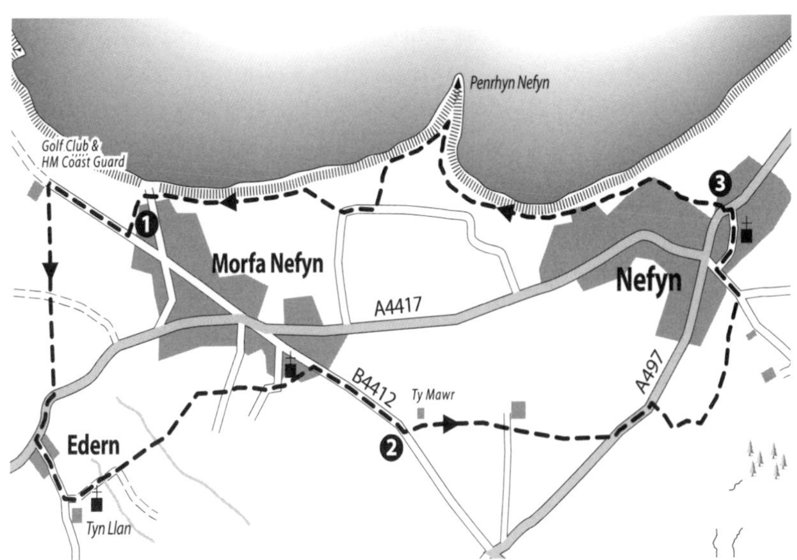

to an old kissing gate in the corner of a fenced field. Go through the gate and walk up the left-hand edge of the field. In the top corner turn right to a kissing gate near a house. Beyond the gate a short track leads to a narrow lane.

Turn left along the lane and pass a small cottage. Immediately after this turn right into an enclosed footpath and follow this to a second lane. Turn left along the lane and in about 75 yards (immediately before the church and cemetery) take a footpath straight ahead at sharp left-hand bend. The path runs beside the cemetery to a kissing gate into a road. Turn left here, then right at the main road (B4412).

Walk along the road out of Morfa Nefyn and just as you leave the houses behind, look for the track to 'Ty Mawr' on the left (immediately before the speed derestriction signs).

2. Turn left down the track passing the house on the left and into an enclosed footpath. Follow the footpath to a kissing gate, then continue ahead along the field edge to stone steps over the wall and hedge. Bear left, then immediately right following a footpath between hedges and walls.

Cross the access road to a house on the left and go through the large field gate opposite and a little to the right. Keep along the left-hand field edge to a ladder stile in the top corner. After the stile, bear right and along the field edge to a kissing gate in the wall on the right just after a farm. Turn left at the main road (A497) and after about 200 yards cross over taking the signed field path on the right. Walk straight across a small field to the edge of a bank overlooking a small valley directly below the wooded Garn Boduan. Bear half-left down the bank on a track to the bottom of the little valley. Turn left onto a footpath which follows the top of a dyke with a small stream on either side. Follow this path to a kissing gate which leads into fields again.

Walk straight ahead up the field to a kissing gate which leads onto a short access track which you should follow to the road. Turn left here, then left again at the T junction ('Stryd y Plas'). Pass a small car park on the right and take the first street on the right. Follow this street past St. Mary's Church with its unusual weather vane depicting a square rigged sailing ship.

The present church was built in 1825 although the foundation is much older. It was closed in 1977 and now houses a maritime museum. In the churchyard are relics from Nefyn's maritime history and a number of gravestones recall those who have perished in shipping disasters on the nearby treacherous coast.

Nefyn's small size and rural character today give no indication of its importance in earlier centuries. It has one of the few examples of a motte and bailey castle in Lleyn and is known to have been used by Gruffydd ap Cynan, father of Owain Gwynedd, as a base in his struggle to gain power.

During the Middle Ages it was the administrative centre of the Dinllaen commote, one of the three commotes of Lleyn, and Edward I's choice of Nefyn as the venue for his tournament to celebrate the conquest of Wales in 1284 gives some idea of its importance at that time. Another indication is the status of 'Free borough' granted by the Black Prince in 1349 to both Nefyn and Pwllheli. A little over half a century later it was burnt and almost totally destroyed by Owain Glyndŵr's rebels,

On the coastal path above Porth Nefyn

possibly because of its growing 'Englishness' caused by burgesses moving into the borough.

It seems Nefyn never recovered from this blow although it remained an important stopping point on the ancient Pilgrims' route to Bardsey. In later centuries fishing became important but by the turn of the twentieth century the once vast herring shoals were gone.

3. Continue past the church to a T junction and turn left into 'Stryd y Felin'. Immediately after the road bends to the left, turn right onto a signed footpath between buildings. At a T junction turn left and follow this footpath down to the coast crossing an access track on the way.

From here you are treated to a fine view of the bay, from the tip of

Porth Nefyn

the headland of Trwyn Porth Dinllaen to the northern slopes of Yr Eifl which fall almost sheer to Caernarfon Bay.

Although there are few ships in these coastal waters today, in the eighteenth and nineteenth centuries they were busy with commercial craft. Evidence of this can bee seen in the numerous wrecks which occurred during these centuries.

One particularly strange tale concerns the wreck of the brig 'Sapho' *which was driven onto rocks at Penrhyn Bodeilas, the prominent headland at the end of the bay to the right and directly below the little church at Pistyll, in 1839. Realising that his ship was doomed the captain assembled his crew and gave each man two sovereigns which they were to keep in a safe place on their person to pay for their burial the next day. When the ship foundered there was just one survivor, a young apprentice who was left the task of arranging the funeral of the captain and his crew who were buried in a common grave at Nefyn.*

The path left follows the edge of the coastal slope for 100 yards or so before you are forced to bear left after a kissing gate. Follow a short path between gardens to a T junction and turn right. Walk along the road with houses on either side and at the next T junction turn right. Almost immediately bear left onto the footpath again instead of continuing down to the beach.

Follow the path along the edge of the coastal slope to join an access road directly above the little hamlet down on the beach at Porth Nefyn. Turn right along the road briefly before bearing right where it bends left to a house. Follow the path to the end of headland (Penrhyn Nefyn).

From here there is a grand view to the northeast of the stepped outlines of Yr Eifl plunging into the sea from a height of over 1,800 feet. These hills provided a barrier to pilgrims en-route from Clynnog-Fawr to Bardsey during the Middle Ages. Their route took them over Bwlch yr Eifl, to the left of the main summit and then down to the little church of Pistyll which sits in an exposed location on the very edge of the cliffs above Penrhyn Bodeilas. From here their route took them on to Nefyn, then along the north coast to Aberdaron. Some idea of just how arduous this journey was in those times is given by the fact that three pilgrimages to Bardsey were said to equal one to one to Rome.

From Penrhyn Nefyn continue along the cliff top path. At the time of writing a section of path has been closed due to collapse of the cliffs. Follow the diversion left to an access driveway by a house. Turn right and at the lane turn right again. Where the lane turns sharp left, go ahead down the driveway to a large house and just before the house bear left onto an enclosed footpath which soon leads to the cliff path again. Follow the path until you are forced to drop to a second beach access road. Directly opposite a signed path will take you back to the car park to compete the walk.

WALK 5

Porth Dinllaen

Distance: 4¾ miles

A delightful walk on gentle footpaths to Lleyn's most unusual and picturesque settlement. In clear conditions there are stunning views of Yr Eifl (The Rivals) across the bay and inland from the end of the headland. Footpaths are excellent throughout.

During the summer the Tŷ Coch (pub) in Porth Dinllaen is an ideal place to enjoy a drink or lunch en-route (open Saturday lunchtime October to Easter).

Start: As for route 3.
Grid ref: 281 407 (Landranger 123, Explorer 253).

The walk

1. Turn right out of the car park and follow the road to the golf club and the 'RNLI House'. Go through the kissing gate onto the golf course and follow the narrow tarmac road across the golf course and down to Porth Dinllaen. Rights of way do exist off to the right as you near Porth Dinllaen but they are not waymarked and it is easier to follow the road.

It is hard to believe, as you walk through this tiny remote hamlet, that in the eighteenth and early nineteenth centuries it was set to become one of the busiest sea ports in North Wales and for a time even rivalled Holyhead as the ferry port for Ireland. During this period it had a shipyard and hotels to cater for travellers and plans were laid for rapid expansion.

This sheltered bay, protected from westerly gales by the long promontory of Trwyn Porth Dinllaen, has long been used as an anchorage and as far back as the sixteenth century ships were regularly unloading here. In 1648 the Postmaster General ordered the Irish mail to travel via Porth Dinllaen instead of Holyhead.

By the late eighteenth century plans were afoot to improve the road from Montgomeryshire to Porthmadog, where William Alexander Madocks was shortly to build his great embankment across Traeth Mawr. This had previously acted as a major barrier to communications, involving travellers in a hazardous crossing of the tidal sands or a long detour through difficult mountainous terrain.

With the new road in place and a recently formed Harbour Company, Porth Dinllaen braced itself for great things. Prospects looked even more hopeful when a Parliamentary Bill was introduced to make Porth Dinllaen the packet port for Ireland replacing Holyhead. Holyhead won the day by just one vote!

This was not end however, with the coming of the railways new hopes were raised and in 1884 a Porth Dinllaen Railway Company was formed and given five years to build the 9¼ mile track to Pwllheli. For some unknown reason this was never accomplished. The isolated location of Porth Dinllaen and the rapid rise of Holyhead sealed its fate.

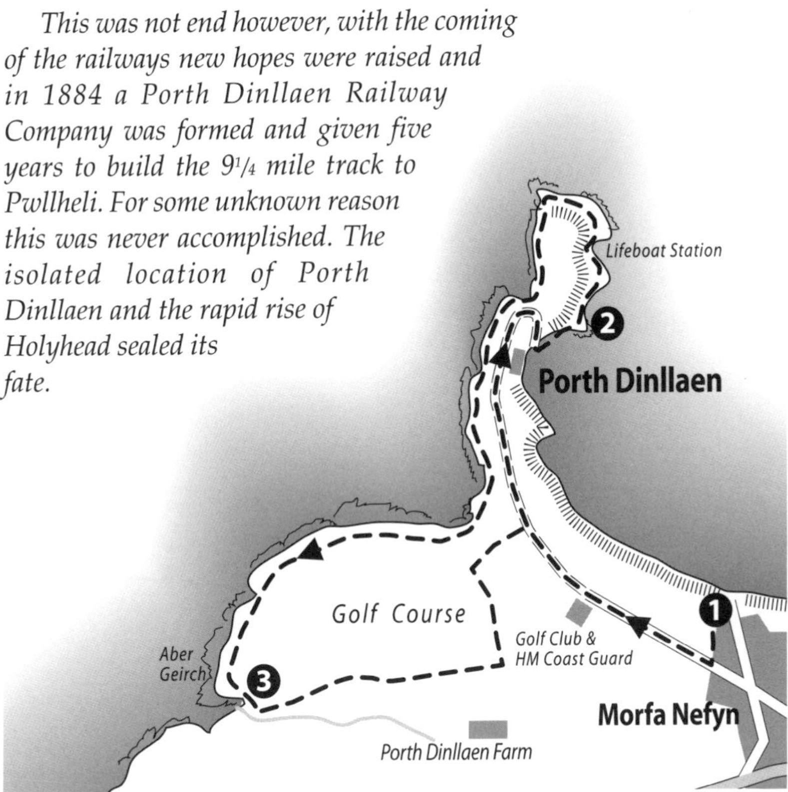

Today we can be grateful for its misfortune—this lovely spot has been largely untouched by the twentieth century. The only boats you will see here today are small pleasure craft. And what a location, safe shattered waters with an unrivalled backdrop of shapely peaks falling sheer to the sea. The robust, stone-built cottages provide holiday accommodation, and where else can you get a pint on the beach! We can only imagine with horror what the effect would have been on this and the surrounding coastline had Holyhead not won the day.

2. Beyond the 'Tŷ Coch Inn' a narrow footpath passes between cottages before continuing just above the high water mark. Pass the lifeboat station and two sandy coves before a slight rise (near a small breakwater) onto a higher path. Continue around the

Porth Dinllaen

coast which is now more exposed and rugged before rising to an old lookout tower.

The lookout is well placed with commanding views of Caernarfon Bay—from Holyhead Mountain on Anglesey to Bardsey on the southwestern tip of Lleyn.

The sheltered bay at Porth Dinllaen is the only safe haven on this entire coast, some 50 miles of jagged rocks and treacherous sands. In 1864, when the first lifeboat station was established, over 200 ships had been lost in the Port Dinllaen area in just 25 years. By 1881 the lifeboat had made 31 launches and saved 91 lives, even so it received public criticism for failing to go to the aid of the 'SS Cyprian'. *This wreck was made famous by the bravery of the captain who sacrificed his own life so that a young stowaway might live.*

The 940-ton 'SS Cyprian' *was commanded by Captain John Alexander Strachan and had left Liverpool on the 13 October 1881 bound for Genoa. By the time she entered Caernarfon Bay a northwesterly gale was blowing and the ship experienced double engine failure. When both anchors were lost she was doomed and preparations were made to abandon ship. While checking life jackets Captain Strachan noticed a young stranger who had come out of hiding and without hesitating gave the boy his own life jacket.*

Shortly afterwards the ship ran aground about 250 yards from the shore near to Aber Geirch and began to break up. Captain Strachan was drowned along with 18 of his crew. Their bodies were buried in an unmarked grave at Edern church and Captain Strachan's body was taken to Liverpool. An inquiry was held at Nefyn by the RNLI where it was determined that the lifeboat could have done nothing to save the crew.

In memory of Captain Strachan, Mrs Noble of Henley-on-Thames gave £800 to the RNLI to be used for a lifeboat on the Caernarfonshire coast. A new lifeboat station was thus established at Trefor. Appropriately the new craft was named 'Cyprian'.

Pass below and to the left of the lookout tower, then keep along the very edge of the golf course. Continue for 1½ miles.

3. At a small bay with a pipeline running into the water, turn inland and cross a stile out of the golf course. Follow the path along a little valley beside the stream ignoring a small footbridge on the right.

Where the path bends to the right go through a kissing gate ahead into fields. Walk beside the fence with a farm away to the right and at the next stile drop into a narrow enclosed path. Turn left and follow the path until it opens out onto the golf course. At the end of the bank on your left, turn sharp right and cross the golf course aiming for a large shed beside the road used earlier in the walk. Turn right and retrace to outward journey.

Yr Eifl from Porth Dinllaen

WALK 6

Tudweiliog

Distance: *5 miles*

An easy gentle section of coastal path typical of this northern coast with a return made by field paths and quiet lanes. Path are excellent on the coastal stretch but the farmland sections are used far less although at the time of writing all stiles and kissing gates are in place.

Start: Begin in Tudweiliog or park in a layby just south of the village on the B4417.
Grid ref: 237 368 (Landranger 123, Explorer 253).

The walk

1. Return to Tudweiliog and about 50 yards beyond the Post Office turn left onto a track between houses, signposted to 'Tyn Llan Caravan Park'. Follow the track to the caravan site and bear right into fields just before the gate. A well worn footpath cuts through the fields to Towyn Farm. Cross the road and take the footpath opposite which leads to the beach at Porth Towyn, one of the few sandy beaches on this exposed coast.

2. Turn left where a sign ('Port Ysglaig') indicates the coastal path, or continue down to the beach and walk along the sand to join the coastal path at the far end of the bay. Follow the coastal path for about 2½ miles to Porth Ychain.

This rocky coastline is exposed to westerly gales and has been a hazard to shipping for centuries. The only safe haven on the entire coast is Porth Dinllaen, hidden behind the sheltering arm of Trwyn Porth Dinllaen. In 1864, when the first lifeboat station was established there some 200 ships had been lost on this coast in just 25 years.

In more recent times, there have been fewer disasters. Today the lifeboat mainly goes to the aid of holiday craft although in 1963 the 314-ton 'St. Trillio' *ran aground near Porth Ysgaden in a southwesterly gale. Launched in 1936 by Liverpool and North Wales Steamship Co. she was en-route from the Bristol Channel to her winter berth at Porth Dinorwic near Bangor when she hit rocks. Three crew members were put ashore by rope ladder including a 21-year-old stewardess who was travelling with the crew of twelve men under Captain Owen Cecil Williams of Bangor. The remaining crew members were able to refloat the vessel on the rising tide and although she was taking in water was able to limp into Porth Dinorwic escorted by the Porth Dinllaen lifeboat.*

3. Bear left where a small valley runs down to Porth Ychain. The path heads inland for a little way before joining a lane beside a white cottage. Follow the lane between hedges and ancient stone walls overgrown with numerous wild flowers.

These low overgrown walls give the fields a measure of protection from the almost endless westerly gales which lash this exposed coastline and allow few trees to grow.

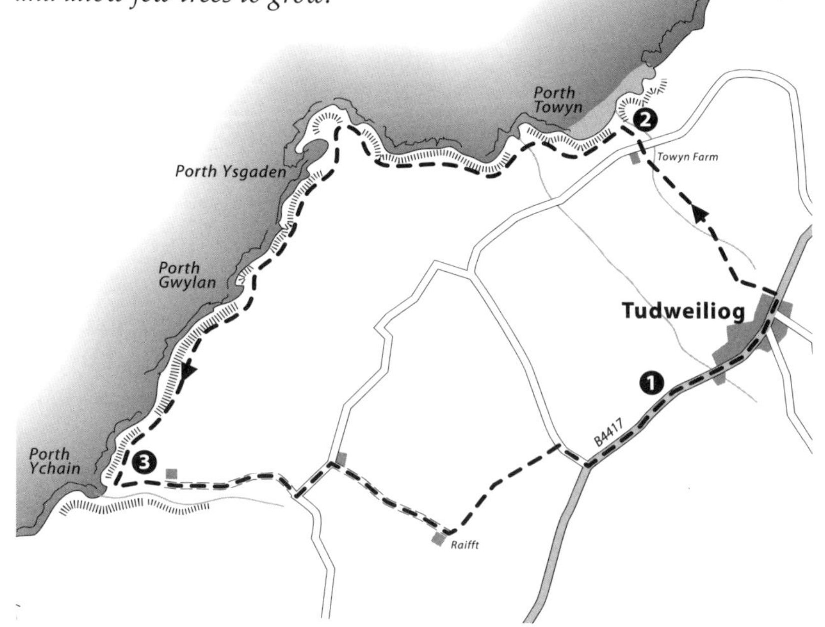

The fine beach at Porth Towyn

Turn left at the road and after about 300 yards look for a track on the right carrying a footpath sign. Follow the track bearing left by a large house on the right before turning left into fields just before a second farmhouse ('Raiffet Bach'). Keep right around the field edge to a stile in the opposite corner. Continue straight ahead now following a line of stiles to the road. Turn right here then left at the B4417 and return to Tudweiliog.

WALK 7

Traeth Penllech

Distance: *4½ miles*

A moderate gentle walk very similar to the previous route. The contrast between the coastal path and inland farm land also applies here.

Start: There is a small free car park at Traeth Penllech reached by following a narrow lane which runs northwest from Llangwnnadl Post Office on the B4417.
Grid ref. 206 341 (Landranger 123, Explorer 253).

The walk

1. Turn left out of the car park and after a few yards take the beach path on the left. This passes through a kissing gate and cuts across fields before leading down to the sand at Traeth Penllech.

This wide bay holds the largest stretch of sand on Lleyn's rocky northern coast and provides fine bathing although it is exposed to cold northwesterly winds. Being largely off the beaten track you are unlikely to find the bay busy except in the height of the summer season.

It was on this stretch of sand that the ironclad baroque 'Stewart' *came to grief in 1901. She was bound for New Zealand carrying a large consignment of whisky when disaster struck; fortunately all lives were saved. At least some of the cargo must have found its way into local farms and cottages to lighten up the long winter months!*

Turn left and walk along the sand until steps on the left lead you back up the slope onto the coastal path. Alternatively, if the tide is low, follow the sand and join the coastal path at the far end of the beach. Follow the path to Porth Colmon where a lane comes down to the water's edge.

There is little at Porth Colmon—a few cottages and a slipway to enable lobster fishermen to lower their boats into the water. Fishing was once an important industry for the people of Lleyn, so much so that it was even blamed for the poor state of its farms. It was certainly true that agricultural interests were put on hold during the fishing season when all attention was given to the catching of herring. The fish were sold fresh locally or, when the catch was large, cured by smoking or pickling and transported to more distant markets. Curing houses would have been a familiar sight lining many of the bays in the Nefyn area during the last century. By the turn of the twentieth century the herring shoals were gone and the industry disappeared.

2. Beyond Porth Colmon, continue along the coastal path for about 3/4 mile.

As you leave Porth Colmon look back for a fine view of the bay backed by the shapely tops of Yr Eifl and Carn Fadryn. Further along

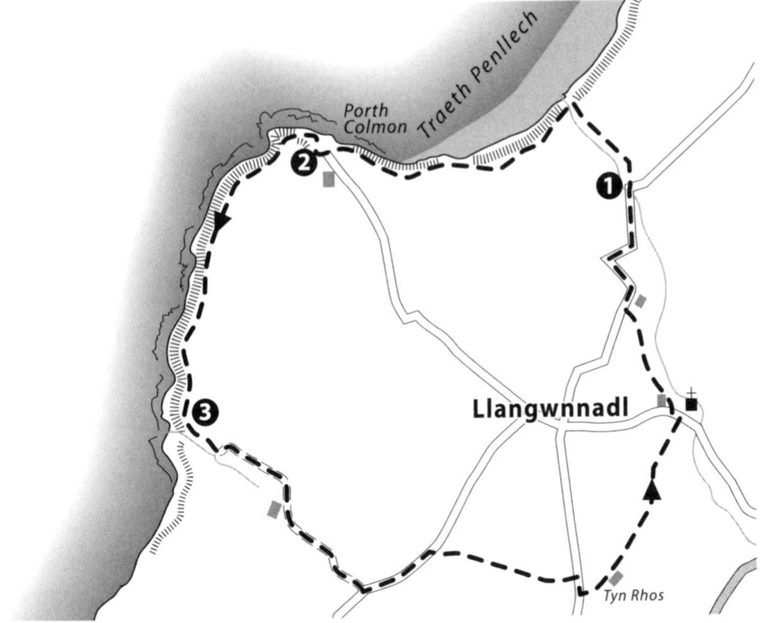

the coastal path, views open out to the south and west to include Mynydd Rhiw and Mynydd Anelog at the southern end of the peninsula.

The terrain along this stretch of coastline is typical of Lleyn—small sheep grazed fields enclosed by low turf covered stone walls. This gives the fields a measure of shelter from the severe winds which blow in from the Irish Sea. Trees are also scarce except for the low stunted bushes which lean dramatically inland and give some idea of the severe winter gales which this coast receives.

3. As you begin to approach a second wide inlet this time without the inviting sand of Traeth Penllech, the path drops into a little valley with a stream; turn left here and follow the remains of an old lane contained between earth covered banks. This is not particularly easy to follow at first and shortly turns sharp left then right. Beyond farm buildings the lane is more frequently used and better defined. Follow this to the road.

Turn left here and look for a footpath sign on the right about 300 yards along the lane beside a small cottage. Turn right and immediately left through a small gate (before main gate) onto a narrow footpath between hedges. Partway along the path a small gate on the right indicates the right of way which cuts through a small field before bearing left through a small gate by a stone cottage. Pass through the garden of the cottage and look for a large metal gate which leads into fields once more. Cut through the centre of the field to a stile, then go ahead through two rough fields diverting here and there around gorse and bramble thickets to a lane. At one point, the path is overgrown in the field corner where the right of way should pass, but a gap in the hedge a few yards to the left seems to have been used more recently.

Turn right along the lane for about 70 yards and turn left opposite a bungalow onto a farm track ('Tŷ'n Rhos'). Adjacent to the house, turn left through a large gate then go right along the wall and beside outbuildings to two gateways in the field corner. Go through the left-hand gate and continue ahead to a stile in the corner. Bear half-left through the centre of the field (towards a house) to a stile in the hedge. Keep along the left-hand field edge to the lane. Turn right to visit the church.

The church, which dates mainly from the 1520s and 1530s is of the perpendicular style and is surprisingly large, being wider than its length. It has a wide naive and two aisles. In the churchyard there are numerous old gravestones, mainly from the nineteenth century including that of Griffith Griffiths who died in 1846 at the age of 93 having lived under 9 sovereigns.

Llangwnnadl is dedicated to Saint Gwynhoedl being of sixth or seventh century foundation and was one of the main resting places for pilgrims using the 'Saint's' or 'Pilgrims' Road' to Bardsey. Its importance continued throughout the Middle Ages and the present rather grand structure (for such a small and scattered community) is possibly an indication that use of the 'Saint's Road' survived into the sixteenth century.

From the church turn right along the lane and just before the old schoolhouse seen earlier, turn right onto a signed footpath. A kissing gate shortly leads into fields and the right of way keeps to the left-hand field edges. Pass through an area of bracken and gorse, later enclosed by hedges, to steps in the wall. In the next field bear half-left through the centre to enter a lane by a stile beside a gate. Turn right now and follow the lane back to the car park to complete the walk.

WALK 8

Mynydd Anelog & Whistling Sands

Distance: *$4^3/_4$ or $1^1/_2$ miles*

An excellent section of coastal path, typical of Lleyn's unspoilt northern coast. This is followed by a rise onto Mynydd Anelog with its wide views to Bardsey Island and southeast across the walled fields of Uwchmynydd. A return is made by farmland footpaths and quiet lanes.

Start: There is ample parking in a large National Trust beach car park at Whistling Sands (Porth Oer).
Grid ref: 166 295 (Landranger 123, Explorer 253).

The walk

1. At the back of the car park take the path behind a large area of bushes. This follows the edge of fields on the left to join the footpath which rises up from the beach.

Whistling Sands gets its name form the curious 'whistling' or 'squeaking' sound which the sand makes when walked on. This is caused by the unusual shape of the sand particles and is achieved by lightly striking the sand with the sole of the foot as you bring it forward with each step. It only seems to work on the hard, partly dried out sand.

Turn left onto the coastal path which is easily followed and keeps close to the edge of the grassy coastal slope with fields on the left for about 1 mile, passing the two islets of Dinas Bach and Dinas Fawr.

There are small sandy coves around these islands which can be reached easily at low tide and make fine picnic spots.

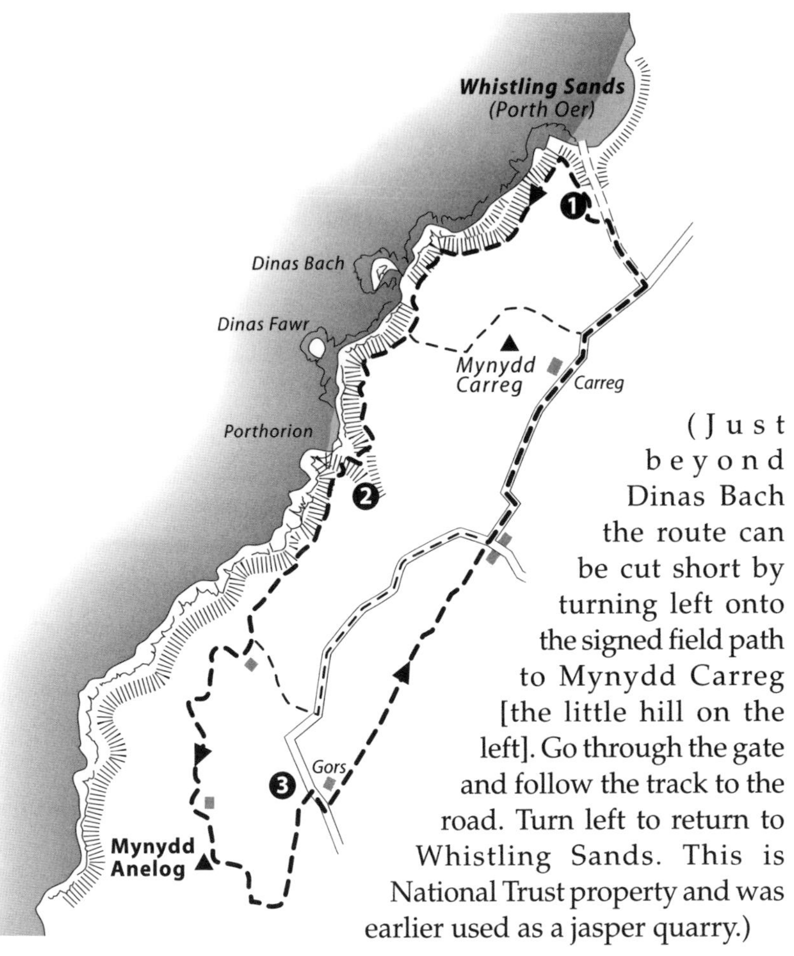

(Just beyond Dinas Bach the route can be cut short by turning left onto the signed field path to Mynydd Carreg [the little hill on the left]. Go through the gate and follow the track to the road. Turn left to return to Whistling Sands. This is National Trust property and was earlier used as a jasper quarry.)

2. Beyond Dinas Fawr there is an inlet and a small but distinct valley running inland—this is Porthorion. A path veers leftwards inland from here, but our way turns right down into the valley to cross the stream by a small wooden footbridge. Cross a ladder stile immediately after the footbridge and rise directly up the slope to the corner of a field on the left. Walk ahead with the field to your left. At the end of the fence keep ahead on the rising path. This path makes its way through an area of rough open grazing land with a small farm away to the left. Eventually a ladder stile leads over a wall. Cross the stile and continue straight ahead on a prominent footpath with fields on the left at first, until you reach a rough track with a small cottage to the left.

(For a slightly shorter round which avoids the climb to Mynydd Anelog, turn left here and follow the track to the road. Turn left and walk back along the lane to the car park.)

Alternatively, turn right and follow the track as it curves leftwards up the hill. Keep right where the track forks and ignore a track on the left soon after. Higher up, make your way towards a small cottage with a wall enclosed field immediately in front. Keep to the right of the cottage, then, at the end of the wall, bear half-left onto a rising diagonal footpath which traverses the slopes of Mynydd Anelog. Pass above the cottage and continue until the two islands at Aberdaron come into view. To reach the summit take one of the narrow paths which rise to the right.

The summit is an excellent vantage point with wide views to the south and southwest of the wall-enclosed fields of Uwchmynydd—the 'Land's End of Lleyn', and the island of Bardsey (Ynys Enlli), isolated by the stormy waters of Bardsey Sound. East lie the wide bays at Aberdaron and Hell's Mouth, while northeast the view takes in the rocky coastline back to Whistling Sands and the headland of Penrhyn Mawr near Porth Iago. The pointed tops of Yr Eifl and Carn Fadryn can be seen in the distance.

This western extremity of Lleyn is characterised by an almost complete absence of trees—only the occasional hardy stump, often leaning dramatically inland, can stand against the harsh winter gales which blow in from the Irish Sea.

Take the narrow footpath which heads in the direction of the two islands at Aberdaron. Lower down rejoin the traversing path above a small cottage and turn right. Shortly, at a sign, turn sharp left onto a footpath which passes through an unusual gate into a small field and beside a second cottage on the right. Continue on the obvious footpath to a gate which leads onto an access track by cottages. Follow this track to the road.

Rising to the coastal path from Whistling Sands

3. Turn right along the road and after about 100 yards, turn left onto a track which leads past a farmhouse ('Gors') and into fields. The right of way now takes a direct line through a number of fields and is well supplied with stiles which mark the route. Sometimes you follow the field edge, sometimes you cut through the centre of the field.

In the last field as you approach outbuildings and houses, cross a stile on the right. Turn left up the field to enter a lane by a stile. Turn left, then immediately right where the lane forks.

The lane can now be followed back to the car park at Porth Oer, but if you want to get off the tarmac as soon as possible, turn left up the track to the National Trust land at 'Carreg'. This leaves the lane immediately before bungalows on the right and farm buildings on the left. At the end of the track a kissing gate leads into fields. Walk ahead down the field to an enclosed footpath which takes you back to the coastal path. Turn right to return to Porth Oer.

WALK 9

Uwchmynydd

Distance: *6½ or 4½ miles*

A fine coastal walk to the 'Land's End' of Lleyn with stunning views out to Bardsey Island. Footpaths are excellent throughout.

Start: Begin in Aberdaron where there is a large car park (fee payable) and WC facilities by the old bridge *grid ref: 173 264.* An alternative start could be made from the free car park below Mynydd Mawr (point 2) situated at the end of the narrow lane leading southwest from Aberdaron (*Grid ref: 141 255).* This option omits the section between Aberdaron and Porth Meudwy. *(Landranger 123, Explorer 253)*

The walk

1. Turn right out the car park, cross the old bridge and pass between buildings ahead to the beach. Turn right along the sand.

Aberdaron is the most westerly village in Lleyn and was traditionally the end of the 'Saint's Road' taken by pilgrims en-route to Bardsey during the Middle Ages. An indication of the difficulty of the journey in those days is given by the fact that three pilgrimages to Bardsey were said to equal one to Rome.

Unfortunately, Aberdaron did not mark the end of their labours, the most hazardous part of the journey, albeit a short one, was yet to come—the crossing of Bardsey Sound. This has proved to be one of the most treacherous stretches of water around the Welsh coast—powerful tide races and hidden rocks can prove fatal even to modern engine driven craft—to the primitive sailing boats of the Dark Ages it must have been a major undertaking. Pilgrims often had to wait several days for favourable conditions both to reach and leave the island.

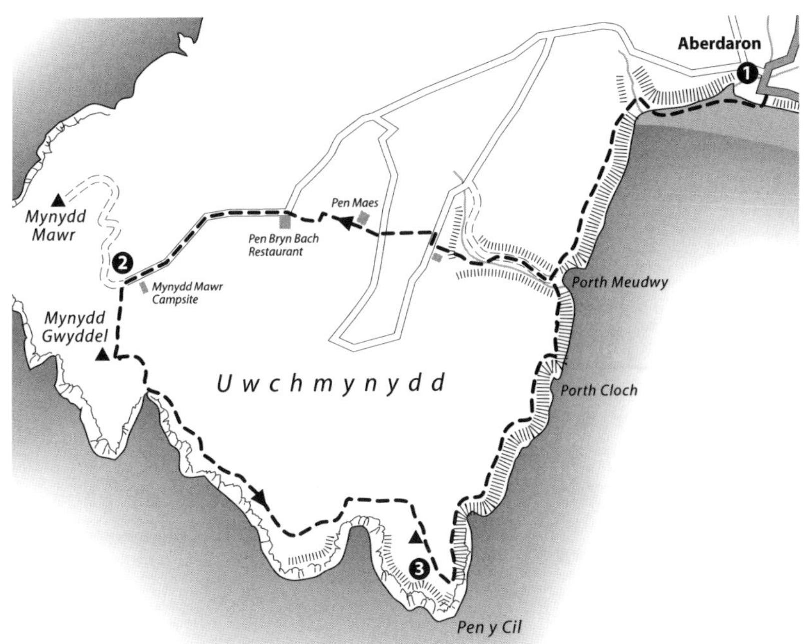

During this period, Aberdaron had many notable visitors, among them Gruffydd ap Cynan, the future ruler of Gwynedd who was given sanctuary by the church canons in 1094 after escaping Norman imprisonment in Chester Castle. They also provided a boat which took him to Ireland before his return to become one of the most notable and long lived Welsh rulers. His saviours seem to have had divided loyalties though for in 1115 they also sheltered Gruffydd ap Rhys of Deheubarth, who was in hiding from both Gruffydd ap Cynan and Henry I.

Probably the most unusual and colourful character to be associated with Aberdaron was Richard Robert Jones or 'Dic Aberdaron', who was born on a farm between Aberdaron and Porth Oer in 1780. Although his parents were probably illiterate, he reputedly learned to speak fluently and write in over 14 languages. His love of foreign tongues and books took him on travels all over the country and his bizarre appearance, dress and unusual talent has turned him into a folklore figure. He died in 1843 at the age of 63 and is buried at St. Asaph church.

Aberdaron church

Ford the shallow river and at the far end of the bay go through the kissing gate and climb steps up to the clifftop coastal path. Turn left and follow the path to Porth Meudwy where steps lead down into the little cove.

Porth Meudwy or 'Port of the Hermit' was one of the embarkation points for pilgrims en-route to Bardsey, being the nearest safe anchorage to the island. Today there are no pilgrims or hermits, just a collection of fishing boats and lobster pots.

Turn inland from here following a track up the little valley between high bracken covered banks. Just before the track bears right and begins to rise, bear left on a narrow footpath to cross a footbridge and rise steeply to a small farm and campsite. Go ahead through the site to a lane. Turn right along the lane and after about 100 yards take the signed footpath on the left between fields. At a second lane turn right then left almost immediately following the track to a stone cottage ('Pen Maes').

Bear left through a kissing gate just before the cottage and go up the right-hand side of the field to a stile in the corner. Cut directly across the next two fields aiming for an old grey farmhouse. Go through a gate beside the farm and follow a track down to the lane with the 'Pen Bryn Bach Restaurant' to the left. Turn left along the lane.

2. Immediately after 'Mynydd Mawr Campsite' on the left and before the car park, bear left on a footpath beside the wall/fence. At the end of the wall bear half-left on a footpath which will take you to the little hilltop of Mynydd y Gwyddel.

This little summit offers extensive views along the coast to the south and inland the hills of Mynydd Anelog, Carn Fadryn and Mynydd Rhiw. Nearer at hand lie the ancient wall enclosed fields of Uwchmynydd but the island of Bardsey two miles across the sound to the west will most likely command your attention.

As already mentioned, Bardsey became the goal of pilgrims throughout the Middle Ages and its claim to be the burial place of 20,000 saints gives some idea of the way in which it was viewed during this period. The pilgrimage is thought to have originated during the Dark Ages when monks from the Celtic monastery at Bangor Iscoed on the River Dee were massacred by the Saxons of Northumbria under the pagan king Aethelfrith, at the Battle of Chester in AD 616. The monks that escaped fled to the safety of Bardsey deep within Celtic lands and the arduous route that these 'holy men' took through what is now North Wales, became enshrined with religious significance which was to last for almost 1,000 years

The first religious settlement on the island is thought to have been established by Cadfan who came to Britain with a company of monks in AD 516 having been driven from Brittany by the Franks. The community that they established was constructed on very simple lines—the monks each had a cell or hut with a small church enclosed by a wall. This arrangement was called a 'llan' and similar settlements formed the base of many Welsh villages as demonstrated by the prefix 'llan' (Llan—gollen, Llan—bedrog) present in their names today.

It is almost impossible for us to comprehend the simplicity of their life on this remote island today, but the monastic community flourished there for 1,000 years and only came to an end with Henry VIII's Dissolution of the Monasteries in 1536. The lands then passed into the ownership of John Wynn of Bodfel who proved to be very unpopular locally and was said have made a fortune by supporting piracy which was rife at the time.

The island is now owned by Bardsey Island Trust who aim to conserve the island's landscape, historic remains and wildlife. One unusual feature of the island is the lighthouse which was built in 1821 and has a square tower.

The well and the foundations of St. Mary's Church which lie lower down to the right are traditionally associated with the pilgrimage to Bardsey, being the supposed place where travellers came to pray before making the dangerous crossing. The lack of a safe anchorage in the vicinity and the greater danger of a direct crossing from here make this unlikely, although the size of the foundation does suggest the existence of a large church or monastic building surrounded by enclosed fields—possibly the home of a second monastic settlement during the medieval period.

Facing Bardsey Island, turn half-left down the hillside to a stile in the wall/fence. Follow the path ahead along the edge of the field to a second stile. After this continue on the obvious path through a more open area.

As you approach a point level with a small rocky islet out to the right turn left and walk up to a stile by a National Trust stone pillar ('Bychestyn') in the upper field boundary. (If you go too far you will reach a deep cliff-lined inlet where you will be forced to turn left. At the fence turn left again to reach the stile.) Go over the stile and follow the field edge ahead to a gate in the far corner. Go through the gate and walk ahead to a ladder stile on the right which leads onto the National Trust property at Pen y Cil—Uwchmynydd's southern most headland. Follow the path to the end of the headland.

There is a fine view from this southwestern tip of Lleyn taking in

Looking across to Bardsey from Mynydd Gwyddel

the wide sweep of Aberdaron Bay with its two islands–Gwylan Fawr and Gwylan Fach (meaning large gull island and little gull island) and the headland at Penarfynydd, one of the enclosing arms of the infamous Hell's Mouth. Look westwards for your last glimpse of Bardsey and the treacherous waters of Bardsey Sound.

From the cairn head southeast down the slope. About halfway down where the slope levels briefly look for a path, faint at first, which traverses leftwards along the slope. Take this improving path soon passing an overgrown wall enclosure on the right.

Beyond Hen Borth, the first little inlet, there are fields on the left and the path becomes more pronounced. Follow this path back to Porth Meudwy and then retrace the outward journey to back to Aberdaron.

WALK 10

Rhiw & Porth Ysgo

Distance: *3½ or 5¼ miles*

A dramatic walk in a little known part of Lleyn. After visiting the remote secluded cove of Porth Ysgo a high level walk over two coastal hills gives spectacular views west to Bardsey and across the wide sweep of Hell's Mouth. Footpaths are generally good.

Start: Begin the walk in the little village of Rhiw, situated high above the wide sweep of Hell's Mouth. At the time of writing Rhiw must be approached by lanes from the north or from the Aberdaron road as the lane near Plas yn Rhiw is closed to traffic. *Grid ref. 227 281 (Landranger 123, Explorer 253).*

The walk

1. From the crossroads in the middle of the village go south along a narrow lane for about ¾ mile with fine views west towards Mynydd Mawr, Mynydd Anelog, Aberdaron and Bardsey Island.

At the gateway to Penarfynydd, a stone-built farmhouse at the end of the lane, you have a choice. Either bear left through the farmyard and continue from point 2, or, for a short detour to the secluded cove of Porth Ysgo, go through the large gate ahead, turn right immediately through a second large gate and walk beside the fence on your right to enter a quiet lane by a stile. Turn left along the lane and about 75 yards beyond a sharp right-hand bend, a signed footpath with two kissing gates on the left leads down a small valley (Nant y Gadwen).

Mining activity in this little valley was begun in the 1820s and continued until 1945 when the mines finally closed. In the final 50

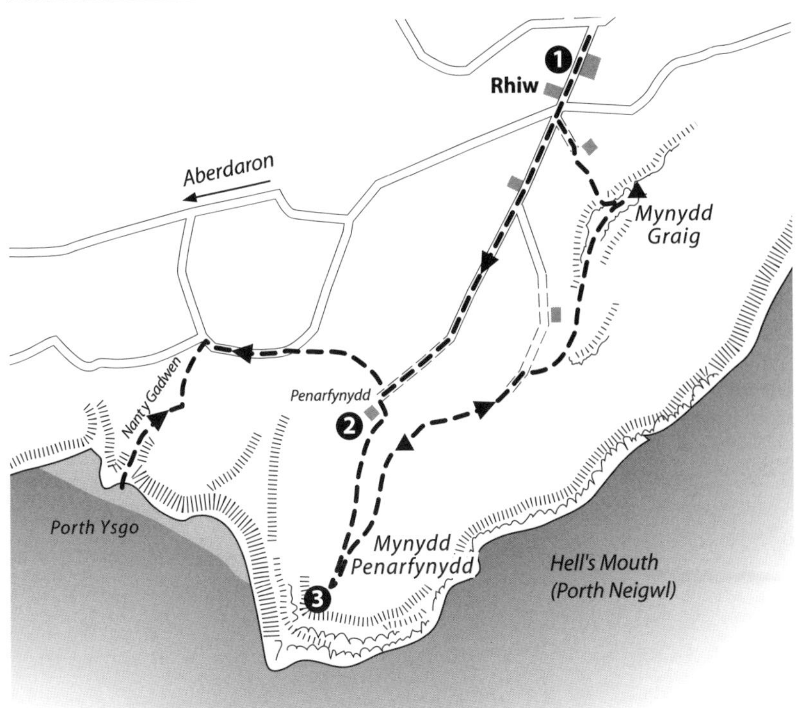

years of its operation 170 tons of manganese were extracted and taken by ship to Liverpool.

At the lower end of the valley, bear right through a kissing gate onto National Trust land. This brings you to the top of the cliffs above Porth Ysgo and a fine view along the coast to Porth Cadlan and the rocky isle of Maen Gwenonwy. Follow the path down a flight of steps to reach the sandy beach.

Retrace your steps to Penarfynydd.

2. At the farm bear right (or left if you did not visit Porth Ysgo) through the farmyard to a gate to the left of the farmhouse. Go through the gate and turn right onto a traversing path. This leads onto the headland at Mynydd Penarfynydd above Trwyn Talfarach.

In clear conditions this exposed headland offers spectacular views of the coast both to the east and west. Westwards, steep cliffs line the coast to Trwyn y Penrhyn, with the two islands of Ynys Gwylan Fawr and Ynys Gwylan Bach (Large Gull Island and Small Gull Island) and Bardsey beyond. Nearer at hand lies the little tidal islet of Maen Gwenonwy, named after the sister of King Arthur. Eastwards the view takes in the wide sweep of Porth Neigwl or Hell's Mouth, enclosed to the south by the green peninsula of Mynydd Cilan. The mountains of Snowdonia line the horizon and lead the eye south along Cardigan Bay to St. David's Head if you are lucky with the weather.

Hell's Mouth became infamous during the age of sail as the grave of literally dozens of ships. Facing the prevailing wind and enclosed by steep rocky headlands it made the perfect snare for ships sailing too close to shore, or who mistakenly thought they had found the safe haven of St. Tudwal's Road. Once within its jaws a ship was doomed.

Reverend William Bingley, writing in 1801 in his book 'North Wales' *described Hell's Mouth in this way: "I never saw a place which presented so favourable an appearance, and that was at the same time so much dreaded by mariners". The natural hazards of the bay were not the only dangers though, Bingley's guide aboard the cutter* 'Flora' *told him: "We remember more misfortunes to have happened in this bay and more inhumanity shown to the suffers, than we have ever heard of anywhere else on the Welsh coast". This is probably a reference to the looting of stricken vessels and the sometimes brutal treatment of those washed ashore.*

One example of this is to be found in the account of a French ship which foundered in the bay and is said to have been carrying a large number of aristocrats fleeing from the French Revolution. Those who survived the sinking and were washed ashore, fell victim to local peasants who robbed them of clothes and jewellery and left them naked and dying on the beach. Such brutality was not as rare as one might imagine, it was not until 1808 that Parliament enacted that bodies washed ashore were to be given a Christian burial. Prior to that, they were frequently left to drift back out to sea or feed the seagulls.

3. Double back now but don't follow the path back to

Looking west towards Bardsey from Penarfynydd

Penarfynydd, instead, take one of the paths which soon fork right to follow the broad flat ridge to the triangulation pillar on the highest point at 580 feet.

Continue northwards along the ridge descending to the field corner where a stile leads over the wall and onto a track by a small sewage works. Follow the rising track towards cottages ahead. Before you reach the cottages look for a stile over the wall on the right. Cross the stile and in a few yards the path splits; take the left-hand path which rises beside and to the left of a small crag. Once on the ridge above the crag follow the broad crest again. Further on, near the highest point (Mynydd y Graig) the ridge crest is lined with small crags to the left.

Like Mynydd Penarfynydd this rocky hilltop gives fine views of the surrounding coast as well as inland to the hills and mountains of Snowdonia. Traces of an Iron Age hill fort have been discovered enclosing the summit but, perhaps because of the natural defences available, they are very minimal and provide little for the untrained eye to see. On the seaward slopes to the north and east, there are numerous hut circles which probably date from the medieval period, while a nearby Bronze Age standing stone demonstrates a long and continuous settlement of the area.

From the highest point retrace your steps back along the rocks to where a ladder stile leads over the wall to the right. Follow the right of way beside the left-hand wall to cross stone steps in the bottom left-hand corner of the field. Turn right now and cross a second stone stile in the corner which leads onto an access drive by stone cottages. Turn left and follow this to a lane. Turn right along the lane and retrace the outward journey.

As you walk down this lane note the large upright stone built into the wall. This has been identified as a Bronze Age standing stone and has evidently been incorporated into the wall at a much later date. The standing stones of the Bronze Age remain a mystery to historians but many have placed a religious significance on them. Perhaps because of this many examples have been destroyed or removed over the centuries while others have simply been incorporated into buildings or walls like this example.

Yr Eifl (The Rivals) from the east

Yr Eifl from the west near Nefyn

The beautiful sheltered bay at Morfa Nefyn (routes 4 & 5)

Porth Dinllaen (route 5)

Porth Dinllaen (route 5)

The walled fields of Uwchmynydd (route 9)

A typical section of the north coast with Yr Eifl in the distance

On the coastal path near Mynydd Mawr (route 9)

Bardsey and Mynydd Mawr from Mynydd Anelog (route 8)

Carn Fadryn and Carn Bach from Foel Fawr (route 14)

Aberdaron (route 9)

Penarfynydd (route 11)

WALK 11

Mynydd Rhiw

Distance: *3½ miles*

An elevated walk on the flanks of Mynydd Rhiw, the highest point in western Lleyn. There are spectacular views for much of the walk. Footpaths are good throughout.

Start: There is a small free car park on National Trust land on the northeastern slopes of Mynydd Rhiw. This can be reach by following a narrow lane northeast from the village of Rhiw for about 1½ miles.
Grid ref: 237 298 (Landranger 123, Explorer 253).

The walk

1. Turn left along the lane and after about 100 yards cross the wall by means of a ladder stile on the right.

As you walk down the field you are treated to a wide panorama of much of Lleyn—a patchwork of fields stretching east to the isolated hill of Carn Fadryn with the pointed tops of Yr Eifl (The Rivals) and the mountains of Snowdonia beyond.

Bear half-left down the field on the obvious footpath between heather and gorse. At a crossing track, cross over and turn sharp right to head diagonally down the field passing a small cottage ('Torbant'). Continue beside the wall on the left to a stile in the bottom corner of the field by a gate. Beyond the stile, continue through bracken to join a track by a cottage on the right.

Walk ahead down the track to a T junction. Turn right here and after about 50 yards bear right onto a narrow footpath which climbs steadily through conifer woods. Stay on the most prominent path ignoring minor paths on either side.

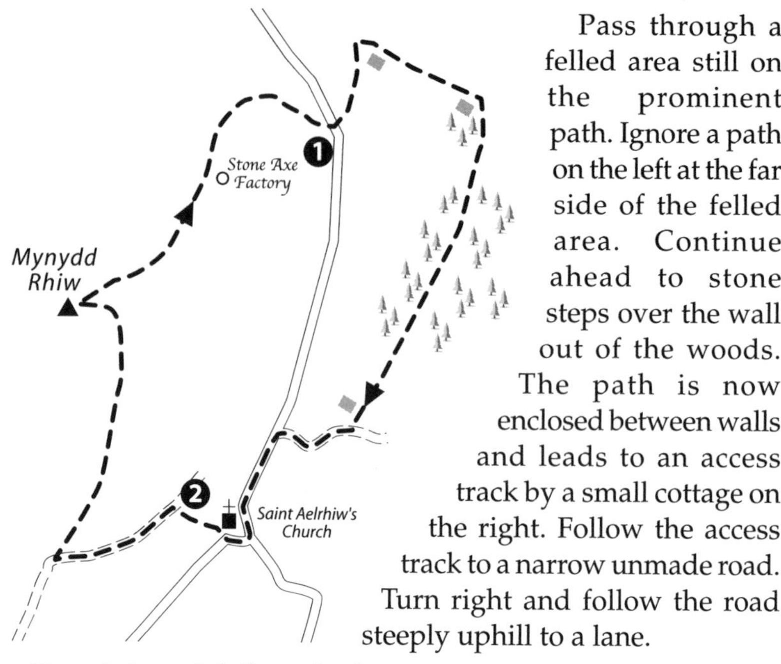

Pass through a felled area still on the prominent path. Ignore a path on the left at the far side of the felled area. Continue ahead to stone steps over the wall out of the woods. The path is now enclosed between walls and leads to an access track by a small cottage on the right. Follow the access track to a narrow unmade road. Turn right and follow the road steeply uphill to a lane.

Turn left and follow the lane past the old church of Saint Aelrhiw.

The church, dedicated to the sixth century Saint Aelrhiw, dates from the eighteenth century but is built on the site of a much earlier building, possibly the site of the original 'llan' or ecclesiastical settlement established by St. Aelrhiw almost 1,500 years ago. A rather curious gravestone bearing a scull and cross bones and dated 1674 is set into the wall behind the font, while a number of soldiers washed ashore in Hell's Mouth during the first World War are buried in the graveyard.

Nearby, set into the hillside and enclosed by walls nine feet square, is the ancient Ffynnon Aelrhiw (Aelrhiw's Well). Wells such as this are often found close to an ancient church and may be the reason for the location of the original llan.

The lane curves around the church cemetery then bends left. Turn sharp right here towards the vicarage then go through a small gate on the left into a sloping field. Bear diagonally-left up the field to the top corner where stone steps lead into a second field. Keep to the left-hand field edge and rise to the top corner where more steps lead over the wall onto a track with the open hillside above.

Looking back now there is a grand view of Porth Neigwl or Hell's Mouth as it became known. It was one of the most feared hazards on the coast of Wales and a ship caught between its enclosing jaws by a southwesterly wind was doomed. The steeply sloping beach is also dangerous and many of those hurled into the water only yards from the shore perished in the surf or were swept out to sea again by strong undercurrents. This makes the beach dangerous for bathing although it provides one of the best surfing venues in this part of Wales.

2. Turn left along the track passing an old cottage and continue until the wall on the left runs close beside the track. On the bend before a pair of cottages on either side of the track, turn sharp right onto a path which cuts through the heather running beneath a line of power cables. Aim for a small rocky knoll just to the

Approaching Mynydd Rhiw

right of a mast on the summit. Higher up, on a bend in the path and as you approach a stone wall coming in from the left, bear left off the main path to stone steps (well hidden) over the wall. Walk ahead to a grass track/path, turn right and follow the track to the summit triangulation pillar (to the left of the aerial).

Take the broad path from the triangulation pillar past the large aerial and drop to a broad grass track. Bear left and follow this path back to the car park.

Lower down, the path passes close to one of the most important Neolithic sites in Wales—the remains of a stone axe factory contemporary with the many ancient burial chambers or 'tumulus' to be found all over Wales. The site consists of five circular hollows ranging from 15 to 50 feet across, with surrounding banks composed of the waste produced by the flaking process. The hollows follow a vein of suitable rock and extend in a line for about 300 feet. When each pit became too deep it was abandoned and a new one started, the debris being used to fill previous pits.

The site was discovered by accident during gorse burning in 1959 and excavation revealed evidence of long use, possibly several centuries, spanning the Neolithic and early Bronze Age. A range of tool types were produced including small knives and scrapers as well as large tree felling axes for the clearing of woodland. Tools produced here have been found as far away as Gwent suggesting a fairly advanced trading infastructure.

WALK 12

Porth Ceiriad

Distance: *5¾ miles*

An exploration of Mynydd Cilan, Lleyn's southern-most headland by means of quiet lanes, bridleways and farmland footpaths. A visit is also made to one of the finest surfing venues in Wales; Porth Ceiriad.

Start: Begin the walk in Sarn Bach near Abersoch. As you approach the village from Abersoch, there is a telephone box and a layby close to the 'Sarn Bach' sign. Park either here or in a larger layby about 200 yards back along the road to Abersoch.

Grid ref: 304 268 (Landranger 123, Explorer 253).

The walk

1. From the telephone box walk south along the road for 100 yards or so and take the signed footpath on the left which passes through the yard of 'Sarn Farm' (to the right, do not enter camp site). Follow the obvious path beyond the farm and at a junction continue straight ahead along a lane ignoring a left fork which leads to a sewage works.

At the next junction you meet a lane which leads down to the beach. Turn left here, then immediately right into another lane. At a crossroads, keep straight ahead again and shortly you will be walking along the edge of the bay with a fine view along Borth Fawr to Abersoch.

The large bay between here and the headland at Llanbedrog is known as St. Tudwal's Road and was widely known during the age of sail as one of the largest safe anchorages in this part of Wales. It was so extensive 'that it would contain the whole Royal Navy of England' claimed one

Stormy conditions at Porth Ceiriad

notable chart maker in 1748. Ironically, just two miles away as the crow flies and beyond the shelter of Mynydd Cilan, is one of the most feared and notorious shipping black spots in the country—Porth Neigwl, better known as 'Hell's Mouth'. The closeness of these two bays inevitably led to disaster and it is not surprising that a number of ships lost in Hell's Mouth had been trying to reach the safety of St. Tudwal's Road and failed to identify the correct bay.

Follow the track until you are prevented from continuing by private property signs. Sadly, there is no public right of way along the coast from here so an inland route must be taken to Porth Ceiriad.

2. Turn right and follow an unsurfaced track past old mine workings on the left.

These are old lead mines and are thought to have been worked since the Middle Ages and possibly even Roman times. What is known about the mines for sure relates mainly to the eighteenth and nineteenth centuries when over 200 men were employed at various times. Flooding was always a problem though and after passing through the ownership of several entrepreneurs, operations ceased in 1895.

Where the track becomes metalled, look for a signed footpath on the left adjacent to a large house, also on the left. Keep to the right-hand field edge and head towards Cim Farm (caravan site). A kissing gate leads onto the farm access road. Turn right past the house and play area. Soon after the play area turn left past a metal barrier into fields again. Bear half-right across the field (towards the roof of another house) and keep to the right-hand field edge passing the house on your right. Go over a stile in the

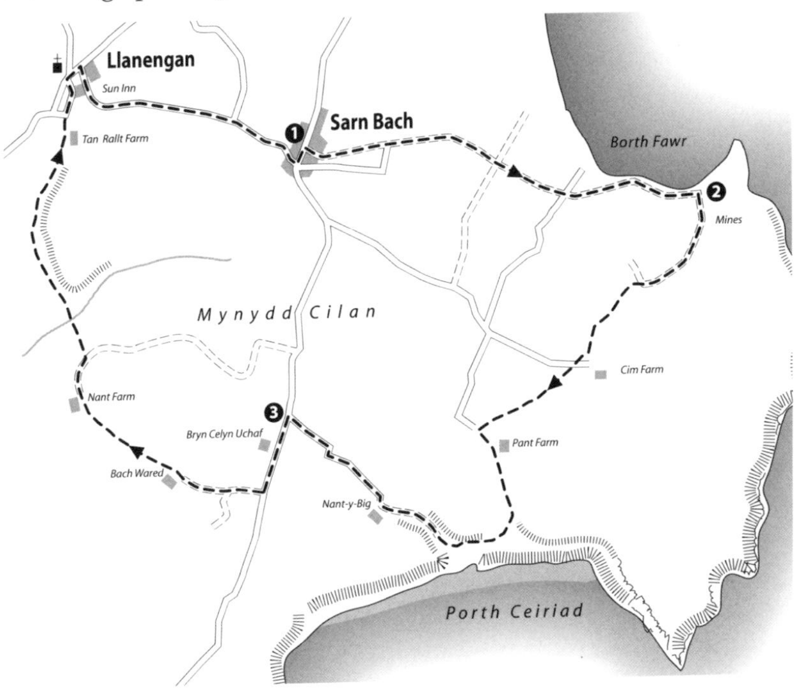

field corner, then bear left between two old gate posts (one fallen, the other standing) and cut through the centre of the following field to another stile. Keep right after this to a stile which takes you onto an access road.

Turn left along the road towards 'Pant Farm' and where the road bends right into a caravan site, fork left towards the farm. Keep right beside the fence to an iron kissing gate which leads onto an enclosed footpath. Follow this path down to Porth Ceiriad.

This cove has something of a fearsome reputation and although safe bathing can be enjoyed in calm weather, great care is needed at times. The beach is quite steep and like nearby Hell's Mouth, experiences some of the best surfing conditions in North Wales.

In 1855 the ship 'Franchise' *ran aground here after losing her position in thick fog en-route to Liverpool. By the time the crew heard the breakers it was too late to turn the ship around. No lives were lost but the ship was smashed to pieces on the beach.*

If you plan to visit the beach bear left to steps by the emergency telephone. If not, follow the path as it curves right, dropping to the flat area at the top of the cliffs. A slight rise brings you to a fingerpost and gate. Bear right uphill as signed beside the beach car park access road (beyond the fence to your left). Eventually a kissing gate leads onto a lane near 'Nant-y-Big'. Turn right along the lane.

3. At the end of the lane, turn left at a T junction and follow this lane passing 'Bryn Celyn Uchaf' farm on the right. In about 250 yards turn right into the next access road and where this forks, keep right through the gate to 'Bach Wared'. As you approach the house, bear right onto a grass bank to reach a stile. Go straight ahead to a second gate, then straight ahead again (keeping to the edge of a little valley on your left) to a small gate which leads into a sloping field. Keep to the left in this field beside the overgrown ruins of the wall and directly overlooking the little valley to the left (which is now quite deep and narrow). Lower down curve right to pass through the yard of 'Nant Farm' by means of two gates. Beyond the farm follow the access track passing a house on the left. About 100 yards beyond this, turn left over a stile and walk directly across the field to a wooden footbridge. Keep straight ahead now (ignore a stile to the left) below a line of small crags on the right. A line of stiles mark the path to Llanengan. At 'Tan Rallt Farm' follow the access road keeping right at a junction to emerge in the village beside the 'Sun Inn'.

Llanengan is a small attractive village arranged around the old church, said to be the finest in the whole of Lleyn. It certainly has one of the most unusual dedications—to Einion Brenin, one of the Dark Age rulers of Lleyn who is reputed to have been buried here.

The stories from this period are based as much on legend as fact, but Einion Brenin is said to have been a cousin of Maelgwyn Gwynedd who ruled much of North Wales from his seat at Deganwy and a descendant of Cunedda Wledig. Cunedda was a Celtic chieftain who came to Wales from the area of Strathclyde with his sons in an attempt to expel the Irish who had been harassing the coastal areas of Wales for a number of years. This he did successfully and in doing so established the kingdom of Gwynedd. After Cunedda's death his sons each inherited a portion of the kingdom, Lleyn coming under the rulership of Einion Yrth. Einion Brenin (or King Einion) was Einion Yrth's grandson.

The church, which can be approached by a small lych gate, is mainly of late fifteenth and early sixteenth century construction and obviously replaced earlier buildings which occupied the site. It was a place of pilgrimage in the late Middle Ages and was no doubt visited by pilgrims en-route to Bardsey as they neared their journey's end. It underwent complete restoration in 1847 by Henry Kennedy although most of the original fabric was retained.

From the 'Sun Inn' turn right along the road and take the first lane on the right. This climbs steeply out of the village before levelling off with fine views back towards Hell's Mouth. At the T junction, keep right and return to Sarn Bach.

WALK 13

Carn Fadryn

Distance: *6 miles*

With the exception of Yr Eifl, Carn Fadryn is the most striking of Lleyn's hills. Its volcanic cone is prominent throughout the entire peninsula and as you would expect, the view from the summit is equally extensive.

This route circles the hill completely before making the modest climb to the summit. The path to the summit is well walked by locals, but to the north and east the rights of way are less distinct.

Start: Begin the walk at the tiny hamlet of Dinas. This lies just off the Nefyn to Sarn Meyllteyrn road about 5 miles south of Nefyn. Park by the chapel.
Grid ref: 269 361 (Landranger 123, Explorer 253).

The walk

1. From the chapel continue to the end of the lane (20 yards) and turn right, signposted 'Llaniestyn, Garnfadryn, Botwnog'. After about 40 yards turn left into a narrow lane contained by high hedges with Carn Fadryn rising directly ahead. The tarmac surface runs out beyond a row of stone cottages and the road becomes a much narrower rough track and eventually a footpath which zig-zags up the hillside for about 700 yards

The path ends at a gate high up on the hillside below the final heather covered slopes of Carn Fadryn with a small cottage on the right ('Pen y Gorgl'). Turn left here soon joining a traversing track for about 25 yards before bearing left to a stile to the left of a gateway just before some ruins on the right. Climb the stile and go ahead through a gap in the wall and along a short section of path enclosed between crumbling stone walls to enter a field. The right of way continues through the fields ahead keeping beside the wall on the right.

Stone steps take you over the walls separating the fields and about 15 yards into the fourth field, turn right over a stone stile in the wall. Turn left along the wall through a young plantation of conifers and at the end of this a stile leads into a large field ahead.

Go ahead through the field. The line of the right of way follows the field boundary on the left but the walked route seems to be directly through the field. After a stile in the fence keep ahead again aiming for a stile almost in the top right corner of the large field ahead.

2. When you reach this don't cross over, instead, turn right and walk along the wall. Pass a gateway and in a few yards cross the wall on the left by a ladder stile. Turn right now and rise through

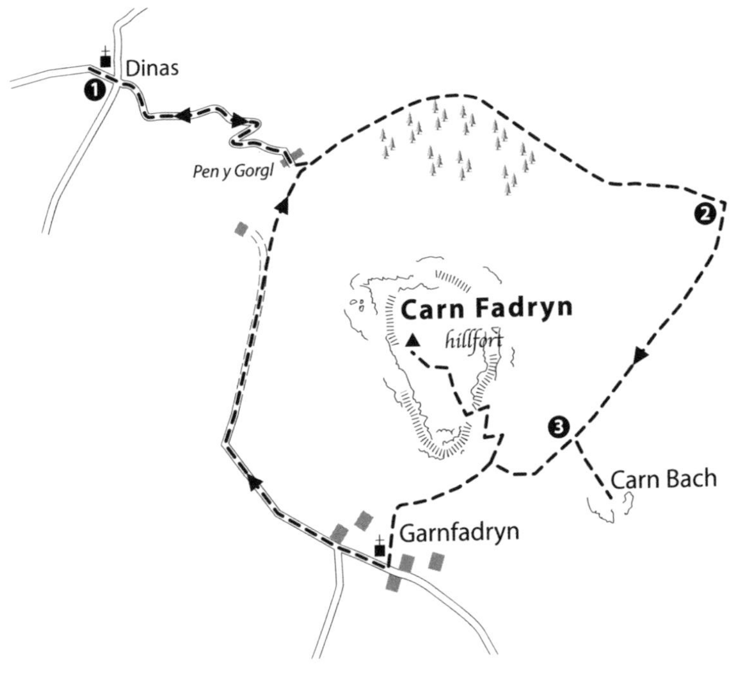

a sloping field parallel to the wall.

At the top of the rise you can see both Carn Fadryn and Carn Bach. Aim for the low point on the saddle between these two summits taking a line which veers away from the wall on your right and leads directly through the field. A gateway should now be visible in a crossing wall just below the skyline and as you approach this you should be able to see a stile in the corner where the wall and the fence to your left meet.

3. Go over the stile and in a few yards cross the wall on the right by stone steps.

(You can make a short detour to the summit of Carn Bach from here by continuing beside the wall instead of crossing the stile. This is access land but you must retrace your steps to this point to continue.)

Carn Fadryn

A large field occupies the col between the two summits. At the outside corner of a walled field on your left turn right to a stile in the wall away to the right. Beyond the stile a faint path rises through the bracken to join the main path which zig-zags to the summit of Carn Fadryn. Turn right and follow the path to the summit.

There are traces on the summit of at least three phases of fortification covering a period of almost 1,500 years. Earliest of these is an early Iron Age dry stone wall defence thought to date from around 300 BC and enclosing around 12 acres. The existence of a cist burial site within the enclosure indicates that the summit was occupied even earlier. A cairn of stones would have originally covered the cist but this may well have been removed to provide building materials for the later hill fort defences.

The next building phase is thought to date from around 100 BC and covers almost twice the area of the earlier phase. There are traces of several hut circles at the southern end of the enclosure and outside the wall to the north. When in use it would have been similar in appearance to the remarkable remains of Tre'r Ceiri on Yr Eifl (walk 1). Like Tre'r Ceiri occupation is thought to have continued throughout the Iron Age and on into the early Roman period.

The latest defences occupy a small area around the triangulation pillar and are thought to be the remains of a twelfth century Welsh castle. The scant remains give little indication of its appearance but it may have been built in the form of a motte and bailey. The Welsh began to copy the Norman style of castle building around this time and the archeological evidence seems to bear this out. There are no contemporary descriptions of the castle in existence but reference to it was made by Gerald of Wales in 1188. In his book 'The Journey through Wales' *he says:*

'We crossed the Traeth Mawr and the Traeth Bychan (the estuaries of the Glaslyn and Dwyryd near Porthmadog). These are two arms of the sea, one large and one small. Two stone castles have been built there recently. The one called Deudraeth belongs to the sons of Cynan and is situated in the Eifionydd area, facing the northern mountains. The

second, which is called Carn Madryn, belongs to the sons of Owain: it is on the Lleyn peninsula on the other side of the river, and it faces the sea.'

This is thought to be the fortress of Maredudd ap Cynan one of the grandsons of the better known Owain Gwynedd. Owain and his father, the powerful Gruffydd ap Cynan, were two of the most notable rulers of Gwynedd. It was Gruffydd who restored the ancient dynasty of Maelgwyn Gwynedd.

The isolated position and central location of Carn Fadryn make the view from the summit one of the finest in Lleyn. Much of the northern coast is visible with the sheltering arm of Trwyn Porth Dinllaen near Morfa Nefyn particularly prominent. To the northeast the hills of Carn Boduan and Yr Eifl (The Rivals) can be seen with the mountains of Snowdonia filling the eastern skyline. Much of Cardigan Bay will be visible on a clear day while the rocky jaws of Hell's Mouth open out to the south.

Retrace your steps down the hillside but follow the path rightwards down to a gate above the village of Garnfadryn. Turn left here and follow the enclosed footpath to a lane.

Turn right along the lane and where it turns left continue straight ahead. After about 1/4 mile the lane deteriorates into two tarmac strips and eventually grass. A little further on look for the cottage passed earlier ('Pen y Gorgl'). Turn left onto the signed path immediately after the cottage and retrace the outward journey.

Abersoch & Mynytho Common

Distance: *7 1/4 miles*

A steady rise up a picturesque valley leads to the scattered settlement of Mynytho and its common land. Broad views can be enjoyed from the common and the optional summit of Foel Fawr. Footpaths are generally good, particularly those sections shared by the Lleyn Coastal Path, but the final sections are less well used.

Start: Between Abersoch and the entrance to 'The Warren' holiday park there is free parking in a layby on the A499. *Grid ref: 316 293 (Landranger 123, Explorer 253).*

The walk

1. From the layby walk south along the A499 towards Abersoch. As you enter the village the road descends a short hill and at the bottom, before a lane on the right, turn right into an access road (between 'Castell' and 'Glenville'). Walk along the road and just before the final house bear right up steps on the signed footpath. Go through the kissing gate at the top of the bank and turn left along the edge of the field. Follow the right of way ahead now along the lower edge of fields with a small valley to your left.

At the end of the fields a stile leads into an area of low trees and shortly beside a small artificial lake on the left. Beyond the lake continue along the valley until your way is blocked by a crossing hedge. There is a gate in the left corner here and two gates over to the right which lead on to farm tracks. Ahead and to the left of the two gates, cross a small footbridge and the stile beyond and follow the path along the base of a gorse covered bank beside the fence.

Cross a stream where the path opens out and go ahead on a rising path between hedges. At an access road bear left and follow this to a T junction with a narrow lane. Turn right up the lane.

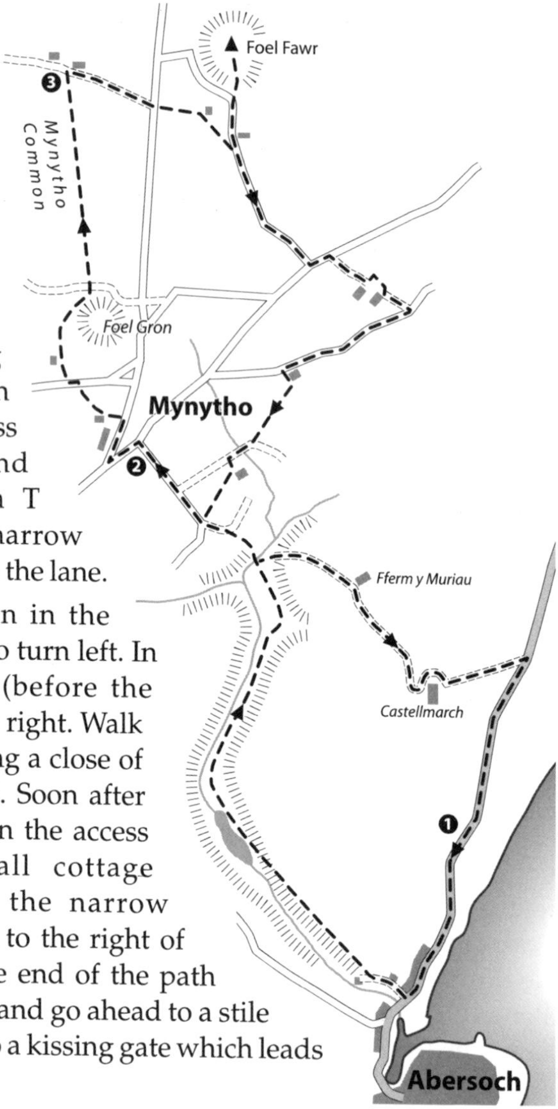

2. At a T junction in the village of Mynytho turn left. In 100 yards or so (before the chapel) turn sharp right. Walk up the road passing a close of houses on the left. Soon after this turn left down the access drive of a small cottage ('Aliwel'). Take the narrow enclosed footpath to the right of the cottage. At the end of the path enter a small field and go ahead to a stile and ahead again to a kissing gate which leads into a lane.

Turn left along the lane for a few yards then cross over and take the signed footpath to 'Foel Gron' on the right. The right of way follows the driveway to a house at first, then continues ahead as a narrower footpath.

Views are beginning to open out behind and left to Abersoch, Hell's

Abersoch harbour

Mouth and Mynydd Rhiw, which forms the right-hand arm of this massive bay.

Where the path forks keep right and a little further on reach a junction of tracks at the southern end of Mynytho Common. If you are in the right location there should be an access track coming in from the right and walled fields ahead and right. Cross the access track and walk ahead beside the wall on the right. You follow a track at first then a narrower path where the track bears left across the common.

As you walk along this path a superb panorama opens out to the line of volcanic hills which run across Lleyn at this point: Carn Fadryn the highest hill is to the left, with the smaller but still shapely tops of Carn Saethon and Carneddol next, and Foel Fawr with its little tower to the right.

3. At a track on the far side of the common near two farm cottages turn right along the track and continue to the lane.

Cross the lane and take the signed footpath opposite. Walk directly across the field aiming for a ruined building in the middle of the field. When you reach the ruin turn right across the field crossing a stile in the hedge/fence. Continue ahead to a stile into the lane to the right of a house.

For a visit to Foel Fawr and its wide views turn left and take the path to the summit where the lane bends left. Return to this point to continue the walk. If you are not visiting Foel Fawr turn right and walk along the lane to the T junction in Mynytho.

Turn left along the road and in about 50 yards turn right down an access drive immediately after 'Talfor'. As you approach a bungalow bear left off the drive and onto an enclosed footpath on the left. At the end of the path go through a gate and turn right along the field edge. Walk through the next two fields to a kissing gate partway along the field on the right. Go through the gate and turn left down a driveway to the lane.

Turn right along the lane and continue to a small crossroads by the chapel. Turn left here and where the access road bends left behind houses and gardens, turn right onto a footpath. This path leads across open common land to an access track.

Turn right along the access track and in about 100 yards or so go left down the driveway of 'Cefn Deuddwr'. Just before the house gate bear right onto a footpath which runs along the top of a 'clawdd' or earth covered wall/bank dividing two fields. At the end of the path enter a lane and turn left down the lane signed for the coastal path. Lower down the lane becomes an access track and where this bends left take the path ahead through the kissing gate.

Descend the enclosed path between hedges (used earlier in the walk) and cross the stream at the bottom of the slope. Turn left now and follow what is at first a faint farm track. As you rise gently the track becomes better established and leads to a farm ('Fferm y Muriau'). Walk through the farmyard and along the access track which passes to the right of the farm house. Continue along the track to the large stone house of 'Castellmarch'. Follow the access road to the main road and turn right to complete the walk.

WALK 15

Llanbedrog

Distance: *4¾ miles*

A steep scramble up onto the open ground of Mynydd Tir-y-cwmwd with wide views along the coast in both directions is followed by easy walking through farmland and along quiet lanes. Paths are generally good.

Start: There is a large National Trust beach car park just off the A499 in Llanbedrog village (parking fee).
Grid ref: 331 314 (Landranger 123, Explorer 253).

The walk

1. From the car park follow the lane down to the beach and turn right along the sand. At the end of the beach walk past a stone cottage ('Foxhole') and continue along the rocky shore passing a second cottage. About 25 yards beyond the cottage turn right up a flight of steps which lead steeply (very) through the trees to the top of the cliffs overlooking the bay.

At the top of the cliffs there is a grand view of the village and bay stretching east towards Pwllheli, while the hills of Garn Boduan, Carn Fadryn and Yr Eifl are backed by the higher summits of Snowdonia to the northeast. The curious sculpture here is known as the 'Tin Man' by local artist Simon Van de Put and supposedly represents the ancient Celts. The original sculpture did not stand the Welsh climate very well, the current structure being a replacement.

Follow the path past the 'Tin Man' and continue round the headland. This area can be rather overgrown with heather and gorse in the late summer although the line of the path is generally clear enough.

Once St. Tudwal's Islands come into view take one of the paths on the right which lead to the triangulation pillar on the highest point of the headland (Mynydd Tir-y-cwmwd).

From here, the highest point on the headland, there is a full 360 degree panorama taking in the curving bays to the east as already described, and west towards Abersoch and St. Tudwal's Island. The northern arc takes in the hills of Mynydd Rhiw beyond Hell's Mouth, Carn Fadryn, the little hill of Foel Fawr with its disused windmill, Garn Boduan, Yr Eifl and finally the mountains of Snowdonia on the skyline. In clear conditions the Rhinog hills and Cadair Idris can be seen across Cardigan Bay. If the clarity is exceptional, the line of the bay can be followed right down to St. David's Head in Pembrokeshire.

These sheltered waters may look inviting on a calm summer day but they hide one of Britain's major shipping hazards, a feature which claimed literally hundreds of vessels during the age of sail—Sarn Badrig or 'Saint Patrick's Causeway'. This curious feature comprises a ridge of stones and rock debris which run for over fourteen miles in a southwest direction from a point about a mile offshore near Harlech. Ships driven into Cardigan Bay by a southwesterly wind became trapped and many foundered on the causeway which dries out completely on

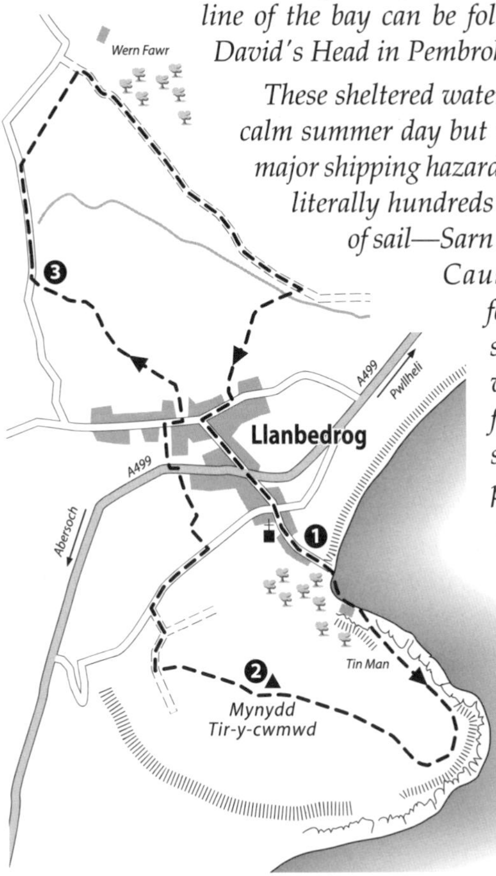

The northeast from the 'Tin Man'

certain tides. The situation was made worse during the eighteenth century by the fact that many early sea charts either showed the bank in the wrong place or omitted it altogether. The charts of Lewis Morris from Anglesey and his son William were the first to give Sarn Badrig its correct location and depth in the closing years of the eighteenth and early nineteenth centuries.

At the end of the headland are the remains of granite quarries established by a few entrepreneurs during the early nineteenth century. Stone was transported by ship to Liverpool and Manchester as well as France for use as road setts. Ships were sailed as high as possible onto Llanbedrog beach at high tide. They were then loaded and refloated on the incoming tide. At the turn of the century the quarries employed around 300 local men, but work ceased completely with the onset of the First World War.

2. From the triangulation pillar a broad path heads northwest (almost directly towards Carn Fadryn and to the right of the hill with the tower). At a T junction turn right and where the track joins a tarmac lane (at a fork) bear left down the hill. Lower down join the old lane from Llanbedrog at a T junction. Turn right here and after about 350 yards turn left along an access track signed 'Public Footpath' (opposite a signed footpath on the right). Follow the track as it bends right and then left between houses. Where a tarmac lane comes in from the right, continue straight ahead on a signed footpath which descends into the trees to the A499.

Cross the road, pass through a kissing gate directly opposite and follow the enclosed footpath between gardens. At a short access road bear right and continue to the road. Opposite, the right of way continues between gardens to enter fields after about 100 yards. Continue straight ahead for about 50 yards before bearing left onto a well worn path between high bracken covered banks. Go through a kissing gate on the right and continue along a small valley.

At the far end of the valley bear left through a kissing gate and follow steps and a rising path to the lane.

3. Turn right along the lane and after about 500 yards look for a stile beside a gate (signposted 'Nefyn'). Cut through two large fields keeping beside the hedge to enter an unmetalled green lane by a ladder stile with the access drive to a large stone house (Wern Fawr) ahead. Turn right and follow an enclosed path between fields for about 1/2 mile.

As you approach Llanbedrog the path over looks a small valley on the right. Just before a farm track joins from the left, turn sharp right onto a descending path. Cross a stile and small brook at the bottom of the slope on the left and rise directly up the bank to a kissing gate. Go through the gate and continue along the field edges (stiles) to a narrow access road. Turn left here, then right at the next junction. Follow this road to a T junction with the B4413. Turn left down the hill and cross the main road by the pub ('Glyn-Y-Weddw Tŷ du'). Walk down the lane opposite back to the car park to complete the walk.

Llanbedrog is an ancient settlement and there has been a church here since the fifth or sixth century when a preacher by the name of Pedrog is thought to have arrived from Cornwall and established the first church, possibly on the site of the present building. This dates mainly from the sixteenth century although parts of the nave could be thirteenth century; a period when churches began to be built in stone for the first time.

The church received rough treatment during the Civil War by the troops of Oliver Cromwell who used it as a stable for their horses. They are said to have destroyed numerous ancient stones in the graveyard and a valuable fifteenth century stained glass window.

WALK 16

Criccieth

Distance: *5¾ miles*

A walk based on the town of Criccieth with its ancient castle. A mixture of farmland, quiet lanes and a short section along the beach with surprisingly good views in some parts. Footpaths are all usable but a little faint in places.

Start: There is a small free car park on the left as you approach Criccieth on the A497 from Porthmadog.
Grid ref: 511 384. (Landranger 124 & 123, Explorer 254).

The walk

1. Turn left out of the car park and follow the footpath down the hill towards Criccieth with the castle standing prominently on its crag overlooking the sea directly ahead.

The castle was originally built by Llywelyn ap Iorwerth ('Llywelyn the Great' or 'Llywelyn Fawr') between 1230 and 1240 to replace a timber and earth castle near Dolbenmaen three miles to the north. He built what is now the inner ward, while the walls of the outer ward and the South West Tower were added by his famous grandson, Llywelyn ap Gruffydd ('Llywelyn the Last'). The castle remained in Welsh possession until it was captured by Edward I in 1283 during his conquest of Wales. Both Edward I and Edward II extended and strengthened the fortress which successfully held out against months of siege during the Welsh rebellion under Madog ap Llywelyn in 1294. This was mainly due to its coastal position allowing it to be supplied by shipping from Ireland; a feature which Edward later used in his castle building. It remained in use until the revolt of Owain Glyndŵr at the beginning of the fifteenth century when it was captured and burnt by the rebels.

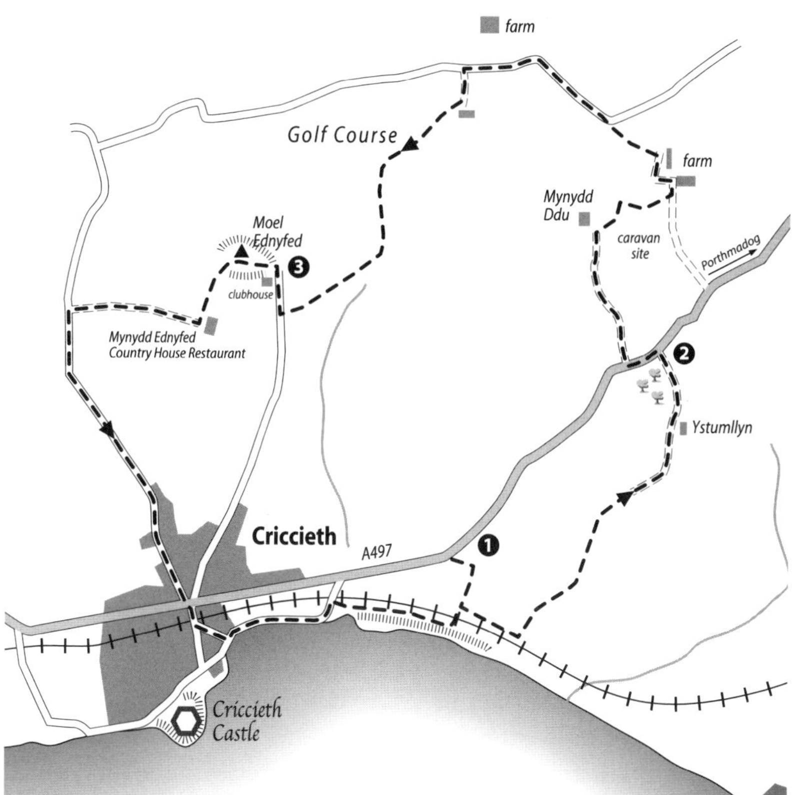

The first recorded reference to the castle was in 1239 when it was used by Dafydd, Llywelyn's son and favoured heir, to imprison Gruffydd, his older illegitimate brother who had become his rival for the rulership of Gwynedd. In 1241, Dafydd suffered a humiliating defeat at the hands of Henry III who forced him to hand over his prisoner. The unfortunate Gruffydd fared little better under Henry's control and died three years later when he fell to his death while trying to escape from the Tower of London where he had been held.

By the time his short rule came to an end in 1246, Dafydd had lost all the territory gains of his father and it fell to his nephew, Llywelyn ap Gruffydd (whose father had fallen from the Tower of London) to re-establish Gwynedd as the main power in Wales. This brought him into direct conflict with Edward I who proved to be one of the most powerful and determined rulers to sit on the throne of England. After Llywelyn's death in a skirmish near Builth Wells in 1282 and the defeat of his brother Dafydd, Edward was able to complete his conquest of Wales.

After about 200 yards, and just beyond the 'Criccieth' sign, take the signed footpath on the left (kissing gate). Descend the sloping field bearing half-left until you can turn right to a level crossing over the railway. Cross the stile but instead of crossing the track turn left immediately and follow a narrow path between the railway lines on your right and the fence on your left.

Just before a rock cutting a stile on the left leads onto a path which rises through a small valley and then passes directly through sheep-grazed fields to join a more obvious track which runs beside a stone wall near farm buildings. Continue straight ahead passing the farm on your left and ignoring a track on your left which leads to the farm. Follow the track to the large farmhouse of 'Ystumllyn' and continue to the road.

2. At the road turn left and in about 100 yards turn right up a rising access road, signed to 'Mynydd Ddu' (Caravan site). As you enter the main site walk ahead and just before two WC blocks, bear half-right through the field to a stile in the far corner. Go over the stile and keep right along the field edge with fine views to Moel-y-Guest, the Moelwyns, Moel Hebog and the village of Pentrefelin below.

In the far corner of the field turn right through a gate and after about 90 yards go over a stile on the left immediately before a gate. Keep right around the field edge to a stile in the far corner. Climb over the stile and turn left along a short farm track to a gate beside a farmhouse. Go through the gate, turn left, then immediately right beside the outbuildings and follow the broad track straight ahead.

As you pass beneath overhead power cables there is a gate angled at 45 degrees to the track on the left. Turn left through this gate and rise to a gap in the top corner of the field. In the following field bear half-right to a gate which leads into a narrow lane. Turn left and walk up the lane.

At the top of the rise look back for a fine panorama which takes in much of western Snowdonia. Particularly prominent are the Rhinog hills which line Cardigan Bay, with Cadair Idris in the far distance. Dominating this view is the fine 'little mountain' of Moel-y-Guest which rises above the marshes of Llyn Ystumllyn, once a small inlet from the sea.

Further on, the lane passes through a small open field with a farm to the right. Continue along the lane for about 160 yards to where fingerposts and stiles indicate footpaths on the either side of the lane. Go over the left-hand stile and follow a track which leads shortly to farm buildings. Pass the farm buildings on the right to a gate ahead which leads onto the golf course (ignore the gate on the right). Cut across the fairway keeping the

Criccieth Castle

clubhouse (immediately below the little rocky hilltop of Moel Ednyfed) directly ahead. Pass through a gate and turn left along the edge of the golf course.

Continue until you reach a small flooded quarry. Turn right here picking up a track which passes between spoil heaps from the quarry. Follow the track to a lane.

Turn right up the lane and just beyond the clubhouse bear left up the slopes of Moel Ednyfed. At the top of the rise look for a gate in the wall which leads onto the grassy summit strewn with boulders.

In clear conditions this little hilltop gives a superb panorama which takes in much of northwest Wales. Below, Criccieth Castle sits on its hill overlooking the bay which stretches east towards the sands of the Glaslyn and Dwyryd estuaries watched over by the rocky hill of Moel-y-Guest. This is backed to the north by the higher peaks of Snowdonia, with Snowdon just peeping over the shoulder of Moel Lefn. Running south from Snowdon you can see Moel Hebog, the pointed top of Y Cnicht (meaning 'the kinght'), the Moelwyns and the rocky skyline of the Rhinog hills with Cadair Idris in the far distance. In exceptionally clear conditions the Pembrokeshire coast all the way down to St. David's Head will just be visible.

Northwards, the western end of the Nantlle Ridge gives way to the isolated and shapely hills of Lleyn—Gryn Ddu, Yr Eifl, Garn Boduan and Carn Fadryn, with the curving bays at Abersoch and Pwllheli.

3. From the summit with Criccieth Castle to your left, drop to a field corner where four walls meet. Bear left here and make your way along the field edge to where a large house is surrounded by trees. A kissing gate in the bottom right-hand corner of the field leads leftwards around the garden boundary. A second kissing gate leads onto the access road to 'Mynydd Ednyfed Country House Restaurant' on the left. Turn right now and take a signed footpath on the left about 75 yards along the lane. In the second field bear slightly right to a kissing gate part way along the wall, then continue on an enclosed footpath between rough walls to an access road. Go straight ahead here and at the

Criccieth Castle from the east

road turn left. Follow the road down the hill and cross the A497 in the centre of Criccieth.

Follow the road over the level crossing and bear left along the water front with the castle to your right. At the far end of the sea front the road bears left to cross the railway. Just before the railway turn right onto a footpath which runs parallel to the rails. At a stile turn left, cross the track and retrace the outward journey to complete the walk.

Mara Books www.marabooks.co.uk

Mara Books publish a range of walking books for Cheshire and North Wales and have the following list to date.

North Wales

Circular Walks in the Conwy Valley
ISBN 0 9522409 7 1. A collection of 18 circular walks which explore the varied scenery of this beautiful valley from the Great Orme to Betws-y-Coed.

A pocket guide to Snowdon
ISBN 1 902512 04 9. A guide to all Snowdon's recognised routes of ascent, from the six 'Classic Paths' to the many lesser known and less frequented routes.

Walking in Snowdonia Volume 1

ISBN 1 902512 06 5. A series of circular walks exploring the beautiful and dramatic valleys in the northern half of the Snowdonia National Park.

Coastal Walks around Anglesey Volume 1
ISBN 0 9522409 6 3. A collection of 15 walks which explore the varied scenery of Anglesey's beautiful coastline.

Coastal Walks around Anglesey Volume 2
ISBN 0 9522409 5 5. A companion volume to the above book, outlining 15 new walks spread around Anglesey's fascinating and beautiful coastline.

Walking the Isle of Anglesey Coastal Path
ISBN 1 902512 13 8. The official guide for the Isle of Anglesey Coastal Path. Full colour in English and Welsh.

Walking in the Clwydian Hills

ISBN 1 902512 09 X. A collection of 18 circular walks exploring the Clwydian Range Area of Outstanding Natural Beauty (AONB).

Walking in the Vale of Clwyd and Denbigh Moors

ISBN 1 902512 08 1. A collection of 18 circular walks exploring the undiscovered country between the Clwydian Hills and the Conwy Valley.

Circular walks along the Offa's Dyke Path

—Volume 1 Prestatyn to Welshpool
ISBN 1 902512 01 4.

—Volume 2 Welshpool to Hay-on-Wye
ISBN 1 902512 07 3.

The first two volumes in a series of three which sample some of the finest sections of this well known national trail.

The Mountain Men
ISBN 1 902512 11 1. This book tells the story of the pioneer rock climbers in Snowdonia in the closing decades of the nineteenth century until the outbreak of World War II.

Cheshire

Circular Walks along the Sandstone Trail

ISBN 1 902512 10 8. The Sandstone Trail is Cheshire's best known and most popular walking route. This book gives a complete route description along with 12 circular walks covering the entire trail.

A Walker's Guide to the Wirral Shore Way

ISBN 1 902512 05 7. A linear walk of 23 miles following the old coastline between Chester and Hoylake.

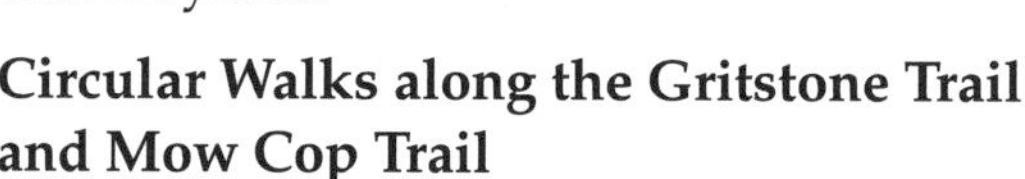

Circular Walks along the Gritstone Trail and Mow Cop Trail

ISBN 0 9522409 4 7. A route which follows Cheshire's eastern border along the edge of the Peak District. Following the same format as the Sandstone Trail book—a full description for both trails is combined with 12 circular walks.

Circular Walks in Wirral

ISBN 1 902512 02 2. A collection of 15 circular walks in the coast and countryside of Wirral.